THE STATE OF

PASTORS

HOW TODAY'S FAITH LEADERS ARE NAVIGATING **LIFE**
AND **LEADERSHIP** IN AN AGE OF COMPLEXITY

A BARNA REPORT PRODUCED
IN PARTNERSHIP WITH
PEPPERDINE UNIVERSITY

CONTENTS

PREFACE

by Dale Brown and Tod Brown,
Research Sponsors

As the world grapples with lingering wars, poverty, injustice, racial tensions and political strife, the Church, the living Body of Christ in this world, matters as much today as ever. Yet troubling trends point to shifting attitudes, at least in the U.S., toward the perceived relevance and value of the Church.

It is no secret that the Church in America is struggling to find its footing in this new environment. We can see it in our empty pews as well as in the data. How should the Church respond? How can we speak into the challenges of this moment? How do we respond to claims, some of them valid, that the Church not only has few solutions to our problems, but that it is *part* of the problem?

Those who are called to lead our churches, whether they are known as pastors, ministers, elders, priests or shepherds, must chart a course through unknown waters. With confidence that the Church will never pass away, pastors can take action to reimagine the role of the Church in our troubled times and find a clear, strong voice to proclaim the hope found only in Christ.

Pastoring a flock of God's people in such a complex season is not easy. The shifting environment places tremendous pressure on church leaders who are trying to make sense of our moment in history and interpret it through the lens of their Christian faith. Some will choose to respond by building a fortress around their church in attempt to preserve the truth of the gospel. Others will venture out into the wilderness of this world and try to spread the gospel's truth. Either way, the path forward is difficult and will test church leaders in new ways.

As we considered how best to serve the Church in this era of complexity, we decided to start by focusing our energy and resources on the well-being and preparedness of today's pastors.

WITH CONFIDENCE THAT THE CHURCH WILL NEVER PASS AWAY, PASTORS MUST FIND A CLEAR, STRONG VOICE TO PROCLAIM THE HOPE FOUND ONLY IN CHRIST

That is why we offered our support to Barna Group and Pepperdine University in their endeavor to understand the current state of the pastor. We were interested to find out how prepared pastors are for their ministries. Did their seminary training anticipate this moment and prepare them for it? How are pastors coping with the stresses of their ministry? Do they perceive their calling in fresh ways or did they lose it long ago?

These and many other probing questions are raised in this study. The final result, presented in the following pages, produces a profile that is simultaneously hopeful and troubling. We were delighted to learn how many pastors still feel a strong sense of ministry calling, but dismayed to learn how many are struggling to lead their church and adequately support their families. Many are weighed down by depression and addiction and feel isolated from the very support systems they extend to the congregations they lead.

THE PULPITS OF
OUR CHURCHES ARE
OCCUPIED BY CREATIVE,
PASSIONATE PASTORS
WHO LOVE GOD AND
DESIRE TO SEE THE
CHURCH THRIVE

This study offers great insights into the hearts, minds and daily reality of those who lead our churches. In the end, we are encouraged by what we see in the findings. The pulpits of our churches are occupied by creative, passionate pastors who love God and desire to see the Church thrive in the days ahead. But behind the hopeful signs are hints of weariness. The margin for some of our pastors is paper-thin.

It is our hope that *The State of Pastors* will prompt elder boards, seminary professors, Christian college presidents and other leaders to examine the support systems that surround pastors and imagine ways to strengthen those who serve today—and more adequately prepare the generation of pastors who will serve tomorrow.

INTRODUCTION

by David Kinnaman, President of Barna Group

I grew up in a pastor's home. I can still remember going to church camps and prayer meetings and Sunday morning worship services. Ah, Sunday mornings. Those marathon Sunday mornings. I acquired most of my social skills in the foyer of my father's church, greeting dozens of people every weekend, trying to match my dad's (genuine) exuberance.

I remember my dad doing so many things right: how he prioritized his family; how he cultivated friendships and hobbies; how, first and foremost, he's always loved Jesus.

I remember the challenges of living in a ministry family, too: not always having money to do things other families did; feeling like everyone was judging what I did and said (especially as a teenager, that sometimes made it tough to be 100-percent myself).

And I remember how leading others and teaching them the ways of Jesus powered and depleted my father in equal measure. I came away from my childhood with a pretty accurate slogan for church ministry: *Where you control nothing and are responsible for everything.*

A LONG LOOK AT SPIRITUAL LEADERSHIP

This project was birthed in part out of my personal experience growing up in a ministry family. Thus, *The State of Pastors* is dedicated to my dad, Gary Kinnaman, to my incredible mom, Marilyn, and to the pastor-parents of the other Barna PKs: Jonathan and Olive Chiu, MaryAnn and Jim Hawkins, and Chuck and Delores Hochmuth. It's a personal labor of love for us.

Beyond family history, Barna brings a great deal of experience to this project: more than 30 years and hundreds of thousands of interviews. We know of no other firm that has conducted such a high volume of research among faith leaders in the U.S. This

THIS REPORT DRAWS ON INTERVIEWS BARNA HAS CONDUCTED AMONG MORE THAN 14,000 PASTORS

report alone draws on interviews we have conducted in recent years among more than 14,000 pastors.

Building on our personal motivations and our company history, a partnership with Pepperdine University and the Brown family catalyzed the 2017 State of Pastors project. They came to Barna with urgent questions about the condition of today's clergy. *How are they doing? What fortifies them in their work? Will a new generation of leaders find their way into ministry?*

To find answers, Barna conducted a new series of national studies among Protestant senior pastors. *The State of Pastors* presents these new findings in light of and in comparison with data we've collected and analyzed over our more than three decades of public opinion research.

The new studies examine three dimensions of church leaders' lives, which correspond to the structure of this report:

SELF
LEADERSHIP

Self-leadership. The questions found in Part I explore pastors' understanding of their interior lives and their feelings about their closest relationships.

CHURCH
LEADERSHIP

Congregational leadership. The questions in Part II probe pastors' everyday experience in ministry and bring to light their priorities, joys and frustrations.

CULTURAL
LEADERSHIP

Cultural leadership. The questions addressed in Part III consider the influence and engagement of pastors beyond their congregation, relying on the perspectives of both church leaders and U.S. adults.

THE WHOLE THROUGH THE PARTICULARS

Here are some things to keep in mind as you read.

Barna's goal for "state of" research is to be as comprehensive as possible. That means, for one thing, capturing a random, representative sample of Protestant pastors across the nation.

This group represents approximately 320,000 church leaders. As you are probably aware, all Protestant pastors are not on the same page theologically or in religious practice (just a little joke, folks). Because our studies include pastors from across the Protestant spectrum, you can bet you'll find some views to disagree with in the following pages. We endeavor not to take sides on issues that divide various church traditions, and trust you can judge the relevance of the findings for yourself and for the people you lead.

We want to be as comprehensive as possible because each dimension of a pastor's life informs and impacts the others. By looking at the particulars in each dimension—self-, congregational and cultural leadership—we believe an accurate picture of the whole (the "state of") can emerge. To shed light on some of those particulars, Barna invited outside voices to weigh in on the findings, and you'll find their contributions throughout this report. It's our hope that their perspectives can help you better understand the internal and circumstantial dynamics that are shaping pastors' lives today.

Which relates to the final point I'd like you to consider: Think about your own context. Do you lead a church? Are you married to a pastor? Do you work within a denomination or organization that trains or supports church leaders? Whatever your role or relationship to pastors, our prayer is that the data you find here will bring clarity to your thinking about how pastors can lead more effectively in these complex times.

It is my belief, further confirmed by this project, that the Christian community in North America does not need stronger leaders; we need *more resilient* leaders. Resilient pastors develop the inner resources and supportive relationships that enable them to prioritize their own spiritual, emotional and physical needs; to view challenges realistically; to learn from their mistakes; to consider alternate perspectives and new processes; and to expect that God is at work even in adverse situations.

We'll dig deeper into resilience later in this report. For now, I invite you to discover *The State of Pastors*.

THE CHRISTIAN COMMUNITY DOES NOT NEED STRONGER LEADERS; WE NEED MORE RESILIENT LEADERS

PART I

SELF-LEADERSHIP

SELF LEADERSHIP

Before he or she is a church leader, a pastor is a human being. And nothing about being a pastor precludes church leaders from the full human experience—good, bad and ugly.

Part I examines who pastors are and how they cope with being human. How do they rate their overall well-being? How many are at risk of burnout, relational breakdown or spiritual problems? What spiritual disciplines help them pursue a deeper relationship with God? How hard is ministry on their families? Do they have close friends? How do they see their financial situation? How do they deal with mental illness or addiction? Are they humble enough to change their minds? And how confident are they in their call to ministry?

The good news is, the vast majority of pastors are personally content and spiritually motivated toward growth and transformation—yet almost every pastor needs greater support in some way from the community of faith. And a small but significant percentage of pastors is at risk in some critical dimension of their lives.

Let's take a look at how pastors perceive their inner lives and closest relationships, and find out how the body of Christ can offer help to shepherds who are hurting.

Most pastors start early on their path to ministry.

More than half sense their calling between ages 14 and 21. Overall, 85% of pastors attended church as a child and 8 in 10 were part of a youth ministry.

A sense of calling deepens with time and experience.

Two-thirds say they feel even more confident about their calling today than when they first entered ministry.

As a cohort of leaders, pastors are getting older.

As other careers woo Millennials and older generations struggle to hand the baton to younger pastors, the median age of pastors has risen from 44 to 54 over the last 25 years.

24% It's not uncommon for spiritual leaders to face doubt.

1 out of every 4 pastors has experienced a period during their ministry when they significantly doubted their faith.

Most pastors are faring well, but 1 in 3 is at risk of burnout.

More than one-third of pastors are at high or medium risk of burnout, and three-quarters know at least one fellow pastor whose ministry ended due to stress.

43% Nearly half of pastors face some sort of relational risk.

43% of pastors are at high or medium relational risk, whether they are experiencing challenges in marriage, family, friendships or other close relationships.

Families usually weather the challenges of ministry.

Pastors report greater marital and parental satisfaction than the general population, though half say their current church tenure has been hard on their family.

1 IN 5 Pastors are not immune to mental health struggles.

One in five pastors has struggled with an addiction—most commonly, to porn— while almost half have faced depression.

Even when earning less, pastors thrive in other ways.

Pastors earn below their education level, but most feel financially secure. High relational, emotional and spiritual satisfaction are found among those making less than $40K a year.

Worship helps pastors stay resilient.

Pastors who experience meaningful worship at their own church are at lower risk of burnout, relationship trouble and spiritual difficulties.

At a Glance

1. IDENTITY

WHO ARE TODAY'S PASTORS?

In 1992 George Barna conducted a landmark study of U.S. Protestant senior pastors aptly titled *Today's Pastors.*[1] This year Barna researchers wondered, *What's changed?* Quite a bit, it turns out.

Pastors are getting older.
In 25 years, the median age of a senior pastor has increased from 44 to 54.

More pastors are women.
More than 97 percent of pastors in 1992 were men, but today one in 11 are women.

Nearly all pastors are married.
This trend is unchanged, actually. But while marriage rates are plummeting among Americans overall, it's worth noting the percentage of married pastors is holding steady.

Fewer pastors have children.
The percentage of pastors with children under 18 living at home has dropped by nearly half in 25 years. This is due in part to the significant increase in pastors' age.

Pastors are staying put.
Average church tenure in 1992 was just four years, and then pastors moved on to a new congregation. Today the average is more than a decade.

Pastors make a livable wage. (Most of them, anyway.)
The annual salary of pastors in 1992 was slightly below U.S. median income. Today the average tops the national norm by a small margin.

1992   **2017**

Median Age **44**

Median Age **54**

Men 97%
Women 3%

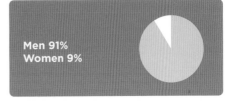

Men 91%
Women 9%

Pastors 96%

All U.S. Adults[2] 61%

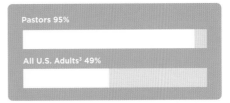

Pastors 95%

All U.S. Adults[3] 49%

66% children
under 18 at home

35% children
under 18 at home

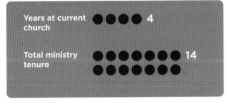

Years at current church   4

Total ministry tenure   14

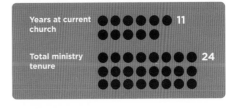

Years at current church   11

Total ministry tenure   24

$46,670[4]	1–10 years in ministry
$56,718	11–15 years in ministry
$60,838	16–24 years in ministry
$59,172	25+ years in ministry

$53,603	1–10 years in ministry
$60,300	11–15 years in ministry
$67,918	16–24 years in ministry
$68,619	25+ years in ministry

Is the aging of pastors a problem?

America's pastors are getting older. When George Barna published his 1992 findings in *Today's Pastors*, the median age of Protestant clergy was 44 years old. One in three pastors was under the age of 40, and one in four was over 55. Just 6 percent were 65 or older.

Twenty-five years later, the average age is 54. Only one in seven pastors is under 40, and half are over 55. The percentage of church leaders 65 and older has nearly tripled, meaning there are now more pastors in the oldest age bracket than there are leaders younger than 40.

PASTOR AGE BRACKETS: 1992 VS. 2017

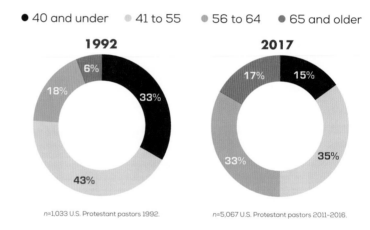

● 40 and under   ● 41 to 55   ● 56 to 64   ● 65 and older

1992
6% | 33% | 43% | 18%

2017
17% | 15% | 35% | 33%

n=1,033 U.S. Protestant pastors 1992.

n=5,067 U.S. Protestant pastors 2011-2016.

The upward climb did not begin in the 1990s. In 1968, 55 percent of all Protestant clergy were under the age of 45—that is, the *majority* of all church leaders were in their 20s, 30s and early 40's.[5] In 2017, just 22 percent are under 45.

There are numerous reasons for this well-documented trend, and it may be impossible to know which are the biggest factors. At the most basic level, people are living longer: Average life expectancy for men in 1968 was 66 years old; today it's 76.[6] More specific to church ministry, the percentage of "second-career clergy" has been increasing over the past two decades, particularly in non-mainline churches* and historically Black congregations; more pastors are coming to ministry later in life, having first pursued a non-ministry career.[7] Additionally, the economic crisis of 2008 impacted pension plans, 401(k)s and home values, and many "senior" senior pastors are not yet financially prepared to forego a regular paycheck.[8]

On the other end of the age spectrum, an insufficient number of young would-be pastors is likely a factor, too. As we explore in "Mentoring" (see p. 86), a majority of current pastors say even finding future leaders—much less mentoring them—is a challenge. It's no surprise that seasoned leaders find it difficult to track down and train their successors when we consider the declining percentage of practicing Christians in each successively younger generation. In addition, even faithful, kingdom-minded teens and young adults are increasingly attracted to vocations other than full-time church ministry, where their desire to make a difference can have a more entrepreneurial expression without the (real or perceived) institutional baggage of church.

THERE ARE NOW MORE SENIOR PASTORS OVER 65 THAN THERE ARE LEADERS UNDER 40

All these factors and more are contributing to the "graying" of America's clergy—a phenomenon with more cons than pros. It's surely an upside that older pastors often have wisdom that comes only with long experience; the Church is in desperate need of such wisdom in this era of unparalleled complexity. Yet God's people also need younger leaders preparing today for an uncertain future. Older pastors are uniquely situated (and called) to raise up, train and release godly, capable and resilient young pastors.

The bare facts of the matter are that even the wisest of older pastors is not here indefinitely, and his wisdom will be lost to the community of faith unless it is invested with the next generation. Even more urgent, however, is the prospect of a massive leadership shortage in the coming decades. In the best-case scenario, Bible-literate, Spirit-filled, missional lay leaders will rise up in the place of a shrinking professional clergy, living as the "priesthood of all believers" (1 Pet. 2:5) on a scale rarely seen before. This is certainly a possibility, but is it the most likely outcome?

* For Barna's definitions of mainline and non-mainline, see Appendix B. Definitions.

2. **WHOLENESS**

How do pastors rate their overall well-being?

Barna asked pastors to rate their satisfaction with various aspects of their well-being, including their spiritual, physical, financial, emotional and mental health. Pastors reported how often they experience a range of feelings associated with contentment or dissatisfaction. This table is a snapshot of how different groups of pastors think about the various dimensions of their lives.

For the most part, pastors present a positive picture. The most common self-descriptions include having a good overall quality of life (91%), ranking spiritua…

Younger leaders tend to rate themselves lower on many dimensions of wellness, and seem to be worse off when it comes to mental health and emotional exhaustion. Yet they are more likely than average to want to become a better leader.

Women who lead churches are more likely than men to say they feel lonely or isolated from others.

Pastors who attended seminary are more satisfied with their financial situation, but slightly less likely than those who did not attend to feel energized by ministry work.

	% All Pastors	Gender		Age	
		% MEN	% WOMEN	% UNDER 50	% 50+
Overall quality of life (excellent + good)	91	91	85	86	93
Spiritual well-being (excellent + good)	88	89	80	80	92
Emotional / mental health (excellent + good)	85	85	82	75	90
Physical well-being (excellent + good)	67	66	72	62	69
Financial situation (secure + surplus)	69	69	67	58	74
Often feel motivated to become a better leader (frequently)	73	74	71	80	70
Often feel well-supported by people close to you (frequently)	68	67	69	66	68
Often feel energized by ministry work (frequently)	60	61	44	58	60
Don't often feel inadequate for ministry or calling (sometimes + seldom + never)	88	89	77	86	89
Don't often feel lonely / isolated from others (sometimes + seldom + never)	86	88	69	83	88
Don't often feel emotionally or mentally exhausted (sometimes + seldom + never)	79	80	62	72	82

Physical well-being increases among pastors with longer ministry tenure.

The difference between mainline and non-mainline leaders on feelings of financial security may be due in part to real differences in income: Median annual income is lower among non-mainline pastors.

well-being as excellent or good (88%) and being in good emotional and mental health (85%). About three-quarters of pastors frequently feel motivated to be a better leader (73%).

Few report frequently experiencing the negative experiences and emotions Barna explored in the study. For example, the vast majority does *not* often feel inadequate to their calling (88%), lonely or isolated from others (86%) or emotionally or mentally exhausted (79%). The areas of health that show some "softness" include physical well-being (67% say excellent or good), finances (69%), feeling well-supported by people close to them (68%) and feeling energized by ministry work (60%). Most pastors are relatively satisfied in these dimensions but, in comparison to other aspects of their lives, contentment is less widespread.

Denomination		Attended seminary		Total ministry tenure			Pastor's compensation			Vocational satisfaction		Satisfaction with current church	
% MAINLINE	% NON-MAINLINE	% YES	% NO	% <15 YEARS	% 15-29 YEARS	% 30+ YEARS	% <$40K	% $40K-60K	% $60K+	% VERY SATISFIED	% LESS SATISFIED	% VERY SATISFIED	% LESS SATISFIED
94	90	92	90	87	91	93	91	90	90	95	79	96	85
89	88	88	88	82	85	94	92	84	87	92	76	92	83
86	85	83	86	74	85	91	89	78	85	91	69	92	77
68	67	69	66	(56)	(67)	(73)	66	63	69	70	58	72	61
76	65	(71)	(63)	61	67	78	56	57	74	75	53	77	58
(66)	(75)	72	76	80	74	67	67	71	76	77	62	80	65
65	68	68	67	64	67	71	(49)	(71)	(70)	78	42	83	51
55	61	58	63	56	58	65	51	58	61	74	(25)	79	38
88	87	87	89	84	88	91	89	87	87	93	74	92	83
82	88	86	87	81	88	89	84	81	88	93	70	95	77
75	80	77	81	74	76	88	79	77	79	88	56	87	69

Pastors who make under $40,000 are more satisfied overall with their lives, except for being less content with their financial situation and less likely to say they are well-supported by people close to them.

The bottom drops out on many elements of well-being for pastors who are least satisfied with their work, even compared to pastors who are struggling at their current church. The most significant gaps are on energy, support from people around them, personal finances and exhaustion.

LIVING THE GOOD LIFE

OVERALL, PASTORS ARE SATISFIED WITH THEIR QUALITY OF LIFE . . .

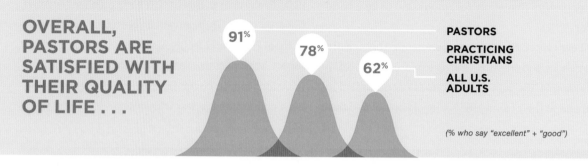

PASTORS 91%

PRACTICING CHRISTIANS 78%

ALL U.S. ADULTS 62%

(% who say "excellent" + "good")

PARTICULARLY WHEN IT COMES TO THEIR PHYSICAL, EMOTIONAL AND SPIRITUAL HEALTH.

(% who say "excellent" + "good")

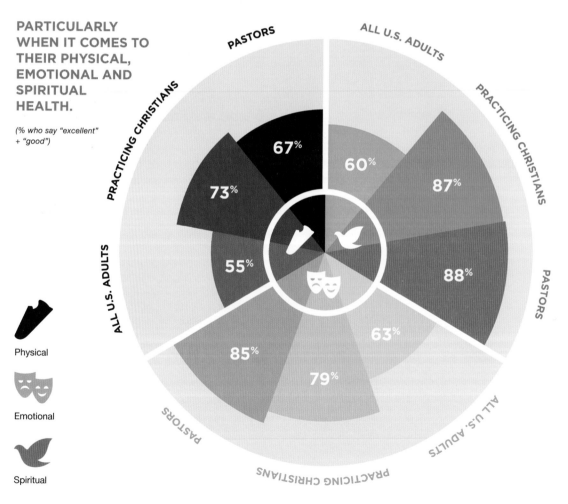

PASTORS

ALL U.S. ADULTS

PRACTICING CHRISTIANS

67%

60%

87%

88%

73%

55%

85%

79%

63%

Physical

Emotional

Spiritual

ALTHOUGH PASTORS ARE MORE OFTEN:

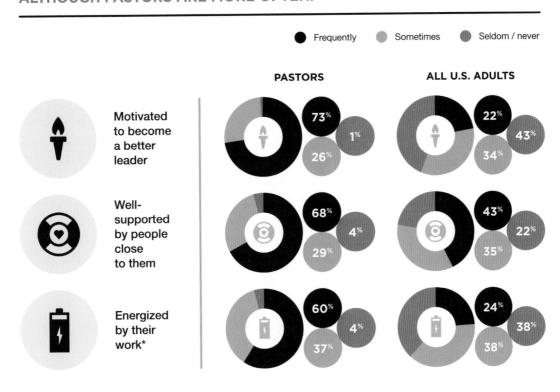

● Frequently   ● Sometimes   ● Seldom / never

PASTORS   **ALL U.S. ADULTS**

Motivated to become a better leader
- Pastors: 73% / 26% / 1%
- All U.S. Adults: 22% / 34% / 43%

Well-supported by people close to them
- Pastors: 68% / 29% / 4%
- All U.S. Adults: 43% / 35% / 22%

Energized by their work*
- Pastors: 60% / 37% / 4%
- All U.S. Adults: 24% / 38% / 38%

THEY ARE ALSO MORE LIKELY TO BE PLAGUED BY FEELINGS OF:

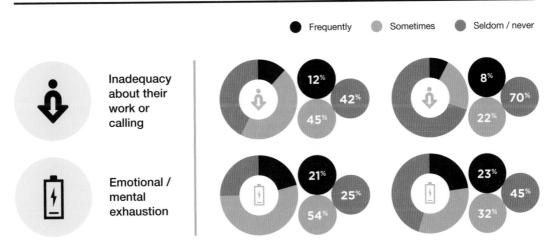

● Frequently   ● Sometimes   ● Seldom / never

Inadequacy about their work or calling
- Pastors: 12% / 45% / 42%
- All U.S. Adults: 8% / 22% / 70%

Emotional / mental exhaustion
- Pastors: 21% / 54% / 25%
- All U.S. Adults: 23% / 32% / 45%

This question asked among employed U.S. adults to compare working pastors with working Americans.

WHOLENESS | **19**

3. RISK

How many pastors are at risk of burnout, relational breakdown or spiritual problems?

While most pastors are doing just fine, thank you, no leader is immune to problems. To understand the challenges to pastors' well-being, researchers posed a series of questions to assess the risk of burnout, relational difficulties and spiritual setbacks. Questions included pastors' self-assessment* of their emotional and mental health; their satisfaction with their vocation and confidence in their ability to minister effectively; the strength of their family and friend relationships; and how they feel about the spiritual dimension of their lives. Researchers then used pastors' self-assessments to formulate risk metrics for burnout, relationship problems and spiritual issues. The items for each metric are shown on page 21.

Numerical values were assigned to all possible answers and, when responses were tallied, researchers found most pastors are doing well, ranking low on two of the three metrics. This underscores one of the major findings of Barna's *The State of Pastors*: Contrary to conventional wisdom, most pastors are faring well.

Still, analysis shows that many are dealing with some level of risk.

- More than one-third of pastors are at high (11%) or medium (26%) risk of burnout.
- Two in five tally high (27%) or medium (16%) on the risk metric for relational problems.
- And while only one in 20 is at high risk of spiritual difficulties (5%)—giving the impression that this is a non-issue for most pastors—an unexpected six in 10 fall into the medium-risk category (61%), suggesting there are currents worthy of notice just below the placid spiritual surface.

---

* Even if there is some self-deception (possible) or aspiration (likely) in pastors' self-assessments, how pastors think about themselves is valuable information.

BARNA RISK METRICS

BURNOUT RISK

- Less confident in their calling today than when they began ministry
- Rate mental and emotional health as average, below average or poor
- Seldom or never energized by ministry work
- Frequently feel inadequate for their calling or ministry
- Frequently feel emotionally or mentally exhausted
- Have suffered from depression sometime during their ministry
- Not satisfied with their pastoral vocation
- Not satisfied with ministry at their current church
- Tenure at their current church has been a disappointment
- Tenure at their current church has not increased their passion for ministry
- Their primary day-to-day tasks do not fit their calling or gifts

RELATIONSHIP RISK

- Rate their relationship with their spouse as below average or poor
- Rate their relationship with their children as below average or poor
- Rate their satisfaction with friendships as average, below average or poor
- Frequently or sometimes feel lonely or isolated from others
- Seldom or never feel well-supported by people close to them
- Say it's completely true that ministry has been difficult on their family
- Report a difficult relationship with their board or church elders

SPIRITUAL RISK

- Rate their spiritual well-being as average, below average or poor
- Say it is very or somewhat difficult to invest in their own spiritual development
- Receive spiritual support from peers or a mentor several times a year or less
- Say their tenure at their current church has not deepened their own relationship with Christ

PASTORS AT RISK

● high risk ● medium risk ○ low risk

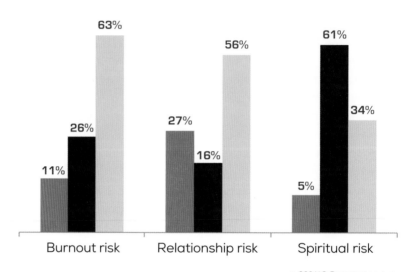

	Burnout risk	Relationship risk	Spiritual risk
high risk	11%	27%	5%
medium risk	26%	16%	61%
low risk	63%	56%	34%

n=900 U.S. Protestant pastors.

Using these metrics, Barna analysts were able to segment pastors into high-risk, medium-risk and low-risk groups in order to see what they might have in common. A lot, it turns out! A substantial part of the analysis that follows in *The State of Pastors* is based on these metrics, because they prove to be helpful in understanding pastors' sense of their overall well-being (Part I), their experience leading a church (Part II) and their perceptions of cultural change (Part III).

THE RISK OF BURNING OUT

Throughout Part I we'll explore various components of pastors' well-being, including the health of their relationships and their spiritual habits. But since a higher risk of burnout seems to play a role in how pastors assess these other areas of contentment and satisfaction, let's take a closer look at the burnout factors at work in some leaders' lives.

Compared to the general U.S. adult population, pastors more often rate their mental and emotional health as excellent (39% vs. 25%) or good (46% vs. 38%). That's more than eight out of 10 pastors who report better-than-average mental health. Leaders of churches with growing attendance (47% excellent) tend to rate themselves higher than those with flat (34%) or declining attendance (22%). This likely indicates that at least some pastors depend on the trajectory of their church's growth for personal affirmation.

Length of ministry tenure also seems to have an effect on pastors' assessment of their emotional well-being: The longer a pastor has been in ministry, the higher they rate their mental health. Conversely, leaders in ministry less than 15 years are twice as likely as the norm to say their mental health is merely average.

> **MORE THAN EIGHT OUT OF 10 PASTORS REPORT BETTER-THAN-AVERAGE MENTAL HEALTH**

EMOTIONAL AND MENTAL HEALTH, BY PASTORS' MINISTRY TENURE

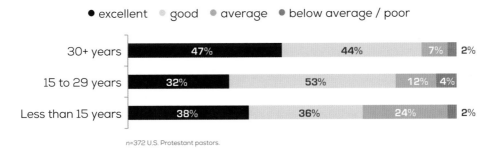

● excellent ● good ● average ● below average / poor

30+ years	47%	44%	7% 2%
15 to 29 years	32%	53%	12% 4%
Less than 15 years	38%	36%	24% 2%

n=372 U.S. Protestant pastors.

Ministry tenure also corresponds to how frequently pastors have felt emotionally or mentally exhausted in the past three months. Pastors with 30-plus years in ministry are less frequently exhausted (37% seldom or never) than those who have been in ministry less than 15 years (13%). Gender is also a factor: Female pastors are almost twice as likely to frequently feel exhausted (38%) compared to male pastors (20%), and are less likely to be frequently energized by ministry work (44% vs. 61% men).

ENERGY AND PASSION FOR MINISTRY, BY CHURCH SIZE

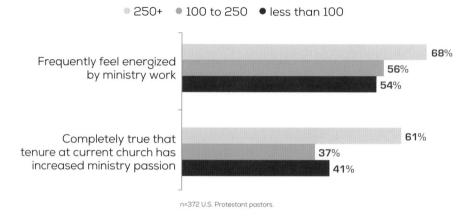

● 250+   ● 100 to 250   ● less than 100

Frequently feel energized by ministry work
68%
56%
54%

Completely true that tenure at current church has increased ministry passion
61%
37%
41%

n=372 U.S. Protestant pastors.

AT LEAST SOME PASTORS DEPEND ON THE TRAJECTORY OF THEIR CHURCH'S GROWTH FOR PERSONAL AFFIRMATION

The larger the church, the more frequently its pastor feels energized by ministry, and the more likely it is for the pastor to report an increased passion for ministry during their tenure at the church. Once again these findings indicate that growth trajectory is a factor in some pastors' positive feelings about themselves and about ministry.

Researchers also found that a church's size and whether it is growing correspond to a pastor's vocational satisfaction, to how satisfied they are in their current position and to whether ministry at their church has disappointed them. Pastors of small and / or declining churches are much more likely than their colleagues to say their tenure as leader of their current church has been a disappointment. About one-third of those who lead churches of less than 100 people (34%) or between 100 and 250 people (37%) say it is completely or somewhat true that their current ministry is disappointing, compared to just 15 percent of large-church pastors. Even stronger than church size is the connection between decline in attendance and disappointment: More than half of declining church pastors say they are disappointed with their current ministry (54%), compared to just one in six of those who lead growing churches (18%).

Pastoral dissatisfaction and disappointment seem to be associated with a church's trajectory of growth. And since dissatisfaction and disappointment raise a pastor's burnout risk, church decline seems to play an outsized role in a pastor's chances of actually burning out.

BURNOUT RISK, BY CHURCH GROWTH / DECLINE

● high risk   ● medium risk   ● low risk

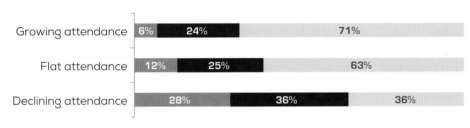

Growing attendance	6%	24%	71%
Flat attendance	12%	25%	63%
Declining attendance	28%	36%	36%

n=901 U.S. Protestant pastors.

Given the unique stresses and complexities of leading a church through periods of intense growth, researchers expected a larger percentage of those who pastor growing congregations to fall into the high- and medium-risk categories. (And it's important to note that a significant three in 10 do so.) Yet the overall direction of burnout risk seems to run counter to what we might expect: Many leaders appear to thrive on the challenges that come with growth, rather than feeling overwhelmed or inadequate.

MANY LEADERS APPEAR TO THRIVE ON THE CHALLENGES THAT COME WITH GROWTH, RATHER THAN FEELING OVERWHELMED OR INADEQUATE

BURNING OUT OF MINISTRY

Barna asked pastors how many fellow pastors they personally know who have left ministry in the past five years because of burnout or stress-related problems. Just one-quarter of all leaders don't know any (24%), leaving three out of four who say they know at least one fellow pastor whose ministry has ended due to burnout (76%). The average (median) number of former pastors known to have left because of stress is two, but one in three current leaders reports they personally know three or more (37%) and one in seven says they know five or more (14%).

Even if we suspect some of these self-reported findings to be on the high side, these numbers are daunting. When we consider than one in nine U.S. pastors is at high risk for burnout based on their own self-assessment, it's not farfetched that most senior church leaders know someone for whom the risks have proven to be too much.

4. PRACTICES

How are pastors growing spiritually?

Considering David Kinnaman's interest in the faith journeys of the Millennial generation, and the degree to which dealing with doubt shapes their lives and faith, Barna researchers wanted to understand what role, if any, doubt plays in the lives of pastors. One out of every four has experienced a period during their ministry when they significantly doubted their faith (24%).

Spiritual doubt seems to go hand-in-hand with the period of adjustment pastors experience at a new church. Among pastors who have led their current congregation for three years or less, one-third says doubt has been a factor in their lives (34%)

Of course, while it is often uncomfortable, doubting one's faith may serve as a catalyst for deeper spiritual growth and more consistent religious practice. For example, pastors with longer overall ministry tenure are more likely than shorter-tenured leaders to report they find it fairly easy to make time for their own spiritual development. The shorter a pastor's ministry tenure, on the other hand, the more difficult it is to find time in their ministry schedule for spiritual self-care.

Those at high risk of burnout (62%) and at high relational risk (55%) also find it hard to make time—or perhaps those who find it hard to make time for spiritual development put themselves at higher risk when it comes to stress and relationship health.

SPIRITUAL DOUBT SEEMS TO GO HAND-IN-HAND WITH THE PERIOD OF ADJUSTMENT PASTORS EXPERIENCE AT A NEW CHURCH

SPIRITUAL PRACTICES

Researchers asked pastors what two or three spiritual disciplines or practices are most essential for their own spiritual development. Eight out of 10 say prayer (81%) and seven out of 10 cite reading the Bible for personal devotions (71%). After that, there is a massive drop off. "Silence or solitude" (13%) is statistically

PASTORS' DIFFICULTY FINDING TIME TO INVEST IN THEIR OWN SPIRITUAL DEVELOPMENT, BY MINISTRY TENURE

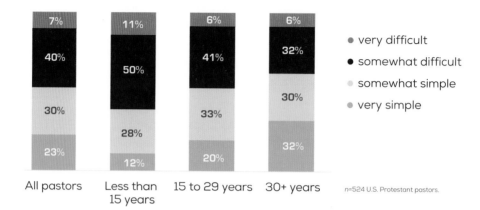

- very difficult
- somewhat difficult
- somewhat simple
- very simple

All pastors | Less than 15 years | 15 to 29 years | 30+ years

n=524 U.S. Protestant pastors.

tied with worship (12%) and "serving others without recognition" (10%) for third place, followed by committing scripture to memory (7%) and fasting (3%).

Demographically speaking, there are not huge variations when it comes to these disciplines; that is, roughly similar percentages of pastors among all ages, ethnicities, church sizes, regions of the country and so on engage in them. Likewise, there does not seem to be any particular discipline associated with greater satisfaction or lower risk metrics.

However, the greater difficulty a pastor has finding time for their own spiritual growth, the less inclined they are to consider reading the Scriptures an indispensable spiritual practice; instead, they are more likely than the norm to value silence / solitude and serving without recognition. Conversely, pastors who say it's simple to find time for soul care prefer Bible reading.

While the specific discipline doesn't seem to have a discernable effect, the consistency of one's spiritual practice correlates to overall satisfaction and low risk metrics. Pastors who are very satisfied with their vocation and very satisfied with their current ministry, or who rate low on spiritual or burnout risk, are most

ESSENTIAL SPIRITUAL DISCIPLINES, BY PASTORS' DIFFICULTY FINDING TIME TO INVEST IN SPIRITUAL DEVELOPMENT

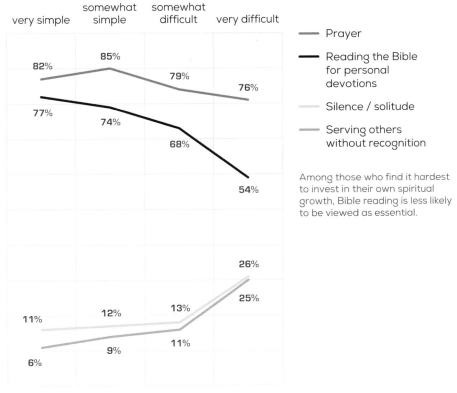

Prayer

Reading the Bible for personal devotions

Silence / solitude

Serving others without recognition

Among those who find it hardest to invest in their own spiritual growth, Bible reading is less likely to be viewed as essential.

n=524 U.S. Protestant pastors.

likely to report practicing their top essential discipline (usually prayer) every day or more often. By contrast, those at high spiritual or burnout risk are less prone to practice every day, and more inclined to do so only a few times a month or less often.

In addition to being the most common spiritual practice, prayer is also the first thing most pastors do when facing a crisis. More than half say they pray first, before taking any other action, when a ministry crisis (59%) or family / personal crisis (52%) arises. This habit is especially common among those who are low on the

THE CONSISTENCY OF A PASTOR'S SPIRITUAL PRACTICE CORRELATES TO OVERALL SATISFACTION AND LOW RISK METRICS

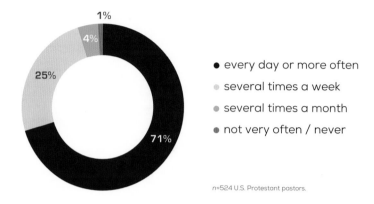

HOW OFTEN PASTORS ENGAGE IN THEIR PRIMARY SPIRITUAL DISCIPLINE

1%
4%
25%
71%

- ● every day or more often
- ● several times a week
- ● several times a month
- ● not very often / never

n=524 U.S. Protestant pastors.

spiritual risk metric: Two-thirds pray first in a ministry crisis (64%) and nearly six in 10 pray first in a family or personal crisis (57%).

MEANINGFUL WORSHIP

As previously mentioned, only one in eight pastors says worship is an essential discipline for their own spiritual growth (12%). Yet a pastor experiencing worship at their church as personally meaningful tends to correlate with a lower risk of burnout, relationship trouble and declining spiritual well-being. Again, it's not clear which way the causal relationship goes—whether higher risk leads to infrequent meaningful worship or less frequent worship leads to higher risk—but the correlation is undeniable.

Similarly, pastors who are very satisfied with their vocation (90%) or very satisfied with their current ministry (91%) tend to report that worship at their church is personally meaningful for them nearly every week.

FIND THE TIME

If pastors and those who support them should take anything from these findings, it's that consistent spiritual practices matter.

HOW OFTEN PASTORS FIND WORSHIP MEANINGFUL, BY RISK METRICS

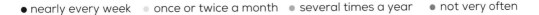

● nearly every week　● once or twice a month　● several times a year　● not very often

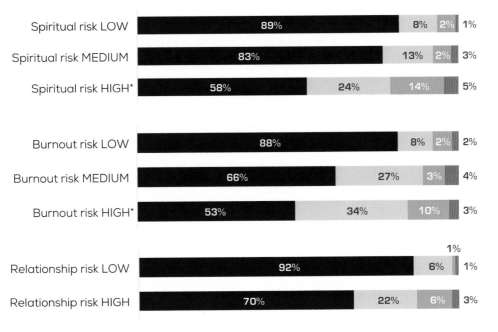

	nearly every week	once or twice a month	several times a year	not very often
Spiritual risk LOW	89%	8%	2%	1%
Spiritual risk MEDIUM	83%	13%	2%	3%
Spiritual risk HIGH*	58%	24%	14%	5%
Burnout risk LOW	88%	8%	2%	2%
Burnout risk MEDIUM	66%	27%	3%	4%
Burnout risk HIGH*	53%	34%	10%	3%
Relationship risk LOW	92%	6%	1%	1%
Relationship risk HIGH	70%	22%	6%	3%

n=524 U.S. Protestant pastors.
*Small samples sizes included for directional purposes.

They matter to the quality of pastors' lives and leadership. They correlate to vocational satisfaction and contentedness with one's ministry. They impact emotional, spiritual and relational well-being.

Pastors can mistake the attention they receive for being a spiritual leader for spiritual maturity. It's not uncommon for congregants to project their unlived spiritual lives onto their leader and call it spirituality. Then, constant praise for inspiring messages and caring deeds can tempt leaders to believe the projections placed on them and call *that* spirituality. This can lead to narcissism that ends in spiritual abuse of the flock, characterized by power and control instead of care and guidance.

It's not wrong or evil for people to look to pastors as spiritual examples (the apostle Paul, after all, told the Corinthians to "imitate me, just as I imitate Christ," 1 Cor. 11:1). But the best defense against the worst possible outcomes of "spiritual projection" is a direct, personal, living encounter with God's Spirit, who "leads into all truth" (see John 14:16). When pastors attend to the Spirit's leading, they are free to live out their calling to lead people into their own encounter with God.*

Pastors who find it hard to make time for soul care are in good company—but that doesn't make the problem any less urgent. It is difficult, if not impossible, to lead people into a transformative relationship with God if leaders aren't engaged with the Spirit in their own transformation. Without the sense of connection with Christ that comes with regular spiritual practice, spirituality can become a job rather than a calling.

---

* Many thanks to Rev. Victoria Loorz for contributing insights on the implications of pastors neglecting to find time for spiritual practices.

Q&A WITH PETE SCAZZERO

Q: In your experience, what are the roadblocks that keep spiritual leaders from finding time to invest in their own spiritual growth?

A: The greatest roadblock, I believe, is a lack of good models. As evangelical leaders, we have inherited a history of activism that goes back more than 200 years. Our great gift is mission: mobilizing believers and leading people to Christ. But this great gift can also be a liability. Spiritually indispensable concepts like silence, slowness, solitude and being (instead of doing) are difficult for most of us who are heirs to evangelicalism's activist impulse. That is why I'm convinced we must learn from the wider Church tradition—Roman Catholic, Orthodox and Protestant—and mine the spiritual riches of our shared history

Q: Why is it important for public spiritual figures to find time for private spiritual practices?

A: Being a leader for Christ without practicing spiritual disciplines that enable us to abide with him is a contradiction. How we can we give what we do not possess? How can we offer the life-transforming message of Jesus if he is not continually transforming us? Regularly practicing prayer, silence, solitude, meditation on the Scriptures, worship, community, Sabbath and simplicity is the door we open to receive Jesus and be transformed by his presence.

Our first work as spiritual leaders is to live *congruently*, which means we are the same person on and off the stage. Our roles and our souls must remain connected; this is our primary work and the greatest gift we can give to others. Without it we have little, if anything, to offer the world in the name of Jesus. And so, the most loving thing we can do for those we lead is to say no to people's incessant demands in order to cultivate a deep personal relationship with Jesus. For this reason, I recommend pastors adopt a personal "Rule of Life" to structure their lives in such a way that they keep *being with Jesus* as the foundation of all their *doing for him.*

PETE SCAZZERO

Pete Scazzero is founder of New Life Fellowship Church in Queens, New York, a large multiracial, international church representing 73 countries. After being senior pastor for 26 years, he now serves as a teaching pastor / pastor-at-large. Pete and his wife, Geri, are the founders of Emotionally Healthy Spirituality, a ministry that equips churches with a discipleship paradigm to deeply transform people transforming the world. He is author of two bestselling books, *Emotionally Healthy Spirituality* and *The Emotionally Healthy Church*, and most recently released *The Emotionally Healthy Leader*. His next project, *The Emotionally Healthy Relationships Course*, will release in late summer 2017.

5. FAMILY

How hard is ministry on pastors' families?

Being a member of a pastor's family has potential benefits and unique challenges. For example, a pastor's child may grow up surrounded by a rich community of believers and mentors, but also may face the scrutiny that often comes with being raised in the public eye. A pastor's spouse may share in the blessings of a nurturing church family, but also may be involved with difficult administrative and relational aspects of the ministry. Barna wanted to know, How do the spiritual, social and financial pressures of leading a church weigh on a minister and, inevitably, their family? And how do pastors feel about their most intimate relationships?

Before we dig in, it's worth reminding readers that these are findings from research among pastors only—not among their spouses or children—so what follows is not a 360-degree view of ministry families. The objective here is to understand *pastors'* perceptions and experience of their home life, which is one important dimension of their well-being.

Let's start with marriage. Overall, there's very good news. Most pastors—96 percent of whom are married—are satisfied with their relationship with their spouse. Seven out of 10 say their relationship is excellent (70%), and one-quarter considers it good (26%). By way of comparison, less than half of all married U.S. adults rate their marriage as excellent (46%), and one-third says it's good (35%). So, by and large, pastors report greater marital satisfaction than the general population. (They also divorce at lower rates: About 10 percent of Protestant pastors have ever been divorced, compared to one-quarter of all U.S. adults; 27%.)

Financial constraints can be a relational burden, yet pastors with leaner resources—perhaps paradoxically—tend to report a stronger connection with their spouse. Those who receive a

SATISFACTION WITH SPOUSAL RELATIONSHIP: PASTORS VS. U.S. ADULTS

% among married Protestant pastors and married adults 18 and older

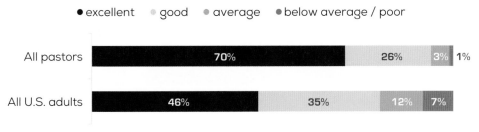

● excellent   ◦ good   ● average   ● below average / poor

All pastors	70%	26%	3%	1%
All U.S. adults	46%	35%	12%	7%

n=490 married U.S. Protestant senior pastors; n=496 married U.S. adults.

lower salary are more likely than those who are financially better off to be satisfied in their marriage. Eighty-three percent of those earning less than $40,000 a year rate their marital satisfaction as excellent.

Pastors with children under 18 (about one-third of all pastors, 35%) are also enthusiastic about their relationship with their kids. Three out of five view it as excellent (60%), and one-third report it as good (36%). Pastors once again rate their relational satisfaction higher than the national average: Among all parents in the U.S., less than half say their relationship with their children is excellent (46%) and three in 10 say it's good (32%).

In a previous study among pastors, Barna asked what, if anything, they would change about how they parented their children. A significant plurality says they wish they had spent more time with their kids (42%), whether that means finding a better balance between ministry and home life, traveling less, being more involved in their day-to-day lives or taking more trips as a family. In some cases, pastors connect these regrets with specific unwanted outcomes: One-third of senior leaders with children ages 15 and older says at least one of their kids is no longer actively involved in church (34%), and one in 14 has a child who no longer considers themselves a Christian (7%).

FINANCIAL CONSTRAINTS CAN BE A RELATIONAL BURDEN, YET PASTORS WITH LEANER RESOURCES TEND TO REPORT A STRONGER CONNECTION WITH THEIR SPOUSE

SATISFACTION WITH PARENTING RELATIONSHIP: PASTORS VS. U.S. ADULTS

% among U.S. Protestant pastors and U.S. adults 18 and older with children

● excellent ● good ● average ● below average / poor

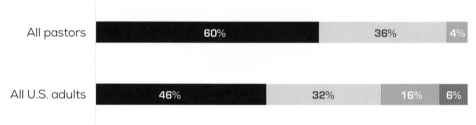

All pastors	60%	36%	4%
All U.S. adults	46%	32%	16% 6%

n=175 U.S. Protestant senior pastors with children under 18; n=601 U.S. adults with children under 18.

Not surprisingly, when it comes to both marriage and parenting, pastors who rate higher on Barna's risk metrics report lower satisfaction with their relationships. For example, pastors who are high on burnout risk are more likely to rate their marriage as average or below average, and to say their relationship with their children is merely average. Likewise, pastors at high spiritual risk are more prone to say their marriage is average or below average, and *eight times* more likely than the norm to say their relationship with their children is average.

FAMILY FIRST

Even among pastors low on the risk metrics, strains of ministry life surface in the findings. Most pastors seem to be doing well overall, but they are not immune from challenges.

Roughly one-quarter of today's pastors has faced significant marital problems (26%) or parenting problems (27%) during their ministry tenure. Pastors 50 and older are more inclined to report either or both types of problems, likely by virtue of their comparatively longer marriages and the fact that many are weathering or have lately survived their kids' teen and young adult years.

When asked whether it's true that their current church tenure has been difficult on their family, two out of five pastors acknowledge it's "somewhat true" (40%). About half say it is either "not very" (33%) or "not at all true" (19%), and just one in 12 says it's "completely true" (8%). Interestingly, these percentages are similar to data gathered by George Barna in 1992 and published in *Today's Pastors*, suggesting symmetry of pastors' family experiences across generations.[9]

A negative impact on family seems to go hand-in-hand with lower ministry satisfaction: Those who report low overall vocational satisfaction or low satisfaction with their current church ministry are much more likely than the norm to say it's true that ministry has been hard on their family. Pastors high on the burnout risk metric also assess higher-than-average negative family impact.

Since the Barna metric of relationship risk is based in part on questions about family life, leaders who rate as high risk obviously tend to report lower family satisfaction. The leading factor that pushes pastors into the relational high-risk category is that ministry at their current church has been difficult for their family. Three-quarters of those at high relational risk say this is completely (41%) or somewhat true (34%), compared to less than half of all pastors. Not coincidentally, relationally high-risk pastors are less likely than those at low risk to express overall satisfaction with their current church ministry: Just three in 10 say they are very satisfied (30%) compared to two-thirds of low-risk leaders (65%).

The data are clear: The effect of ministry on a pastor's family, whether positive or negative, is tied to the pastor's ministry satisfaction.

THE LEADING FACTOR THAT PUSHES PASTORS INTO THE RELATIONAL HIGH-RISK CATEGORY IS THAT MINISTRY AT THEIR CURRENT CHURCH HAS BEEN HARD ON THEIR FAMILY

6. FRIENDS
PASTORS AND FRIENDSHIP

Compared to their high levels of family satisfaction, pastors' feelings on friends are more mixed.

Pastors are a little more likely to be satisfied with their friendships.
Rank their satisfaction level for "having true friends" as excellent

And more often feel supported by those close to them.
Have "frequently" felt supported by those close to them in the past three months

HOWEVER, PASTORS ARE ALSO MORE LIKELY THAN THE GENERAL POPULATION TO FEEL LONELY AND ISOLATED FROM OTHERS

Perhaps because of the nature of their work—which can serve to set pastors apart from those they minister to and even from their peers—pastors report feeling lonely more often than most adults. They are much less likely to say they "never" feel lonely.

How often, in the past three months, have you felt lonely or isolated from others?

- ● Pastors
- ● All adults

  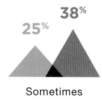  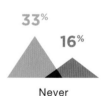

Frequently	Sometimes	Seldom	Never
14% 14%	25% 38%	28% 32%	33% 16%

GEN-XERS: THE OUTLIERS

Pastors in their 30s and 40s seem to have a harder time making friends and feeling connected— they're more similar to Gen-Xers in the general population than to their colleagues in ministry.

HIGHEST LEVEL OF SATISFACTION WITH HAVING TRUE FRIENDS

All adults	Gen-Xers	Gen-Xer pastors	All pastors
28%	25%	23%	34%

Do pastors have close friends?

Previous Barna studies have indicated some difficulties for church leaders, historically speaking, when it comes to making and maintaining close friendships, so researchers were pleasantly surprised to hear mostly positive reports from pastors: Two-thirds are happy with their friendships, rating their satisfaction in the friend department as either excellent (34%) or good (33%).

However, there are some areas of concern when it comes to pastors and the friends they keep. First, note that only one-third of pastors expresses the strongest level of satisfaction with their friendships. Second, around one in three indicates comparatively low satisfaction in this area. And third, pastors' satisfaction with friends is on par with or only slightly better than U.S. adults overall (28% excellent, 33% good)—which raises the question why people in such a relationally driven vocation are not any better than the norm when it comes to intimacy with friends.

Further analysis also shows that robust and healthy friendships are not evenly distributed throughout the pastor population. Overall, older and more seasoned ministers report higher levels of satisfaction than younger and greener pastors. Those 50 and older are more likely to rate their satisfaction with "having true friends" as excellent and less likely to rate it below average or poor. Similarly, those who have been in ministry 30 years or longer or at their current church 10 or more years characterize the state of their friendships as excellent more often than the norm.

It may be that younger pastors, who are establishing not only their ministry but also their marriage and family, have limited relational resources to invest in close friendships. Older and established leaders, on the other hand, may have more relational availability, a clearer sense of their own identity and more opportunities to form friendships based on shared interests, rather than life stage or convenient proximity.

PASTORS' SATISFACTION WITH THEIR FRIENDSHIPS IS ON PAR WITH OR ONLY SLIGHTLY BETTER THAN U.S. ADULTS OVERALL

SATISFACTION WITH "HAVING TRUE FRIENDS"

● excellent   ● good

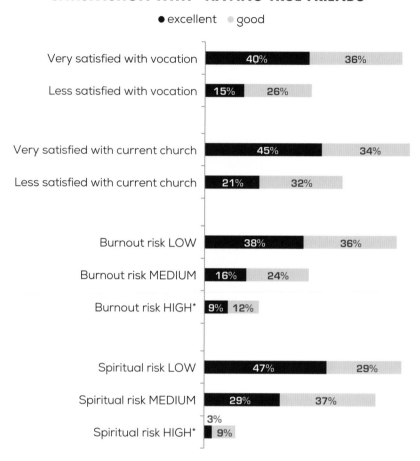

Very satisfied with vocation: **40%** · 36%

Less satisfied with vocation: **15%** · 26%

Very satisfied with current church: **45%** · 34%

Less satisfied with current church: **21%** · 32%

Burnout risk LOW: **38%** · 36%

Burnout risk MEDIUM: **16%** · 24%

Burnout risk HIGH*: **9%** · 12%

Spiritual risk LOW: **47%** · 29%

Spiritual risk MEDIUM: **29%** · 37%

Spiritual risk HIGH*: 3% · **9%**

n=524 U.S. Protestant pastors.
*Small samples sizes included for directional purposes.

Leaders making less than $40,000 per year are also more likely to report high satisfaction when it comes to friends—interestingly, this group also tends to be more satisfied with their family relationships than their higher-paid peers.

When it comes to having true friends, there are dramatic differences between pastors who say they are satisfied with their church and vocation and those who are not, and between leaders who fall at various points along the spiritual and burnout risk metrics. The correlations between higher friendship satisfaction and lower overall risk make a compelling case for the necessity of genuine friendships among pastors.

SUPPORT NETWORK

Barna also asked pastors how often they receive personal spiritual support, either from peers or from a mentor. Again, there was better news than expected. Most pastors are not left alone to fend for themselves: Nearly seven in 10 say they receive direct support at least monthly (68%), and more than half of those do so "several times a month or more often" (37%).

As with pastors' reports of satisfying friendships, there are some differences when it comes to ministry tenure—only on this

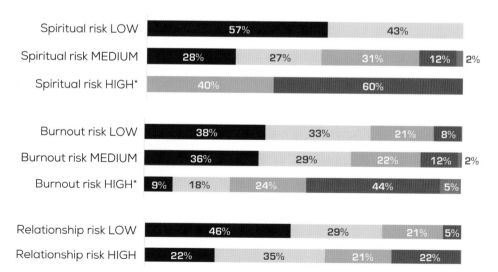

FREQUENCY OF PEER / MENTOR SPIRITUAL SUPPORT, BY PASTORS' RISK METRICS

● several times a month+   ● not very often
● once or twice a month   ● never
● several times a year

Spiritual risk LOW	57%	43%	
Spiritual risk MEDIUM	28% 27% 31% 12%	2%	
Spiritual risk HIGH*	40% 60%		
Burnout risk LOW	38% 33% 21% 8%		
Burnout risk MEDIUM	36% 29% 22% 12%	2%	
Burnout risk HIGH*	9% 18% 24% 44% 5%		
Relationship risk LOW	46% 29% 21% 5%		
Relationship risk HIGH	22% 35% 21% 22%		

n=525 U.S. Protestant pastors.
*Small samples sizes included for directional purposes.

question, younger and greener pastors tend to say they receive more frequent support. (Perhaps this is because older, veteran leaders are more likely to be mentors than mentees.)

Once again, however, the greatest disparities can be found between those who are high and low on the Barna risk metrics. Low-risk pastors receive personal spiritual support far more often than those who qualify as high-risk.

As with other questions from the study that strongly correlate to high measures of risk, it's difficult to determine whether a lack of healthy, spiritually supportive friendships leads to greater spiritual, relational and burnout risk, or the other way around—or whether the dynamic is more complex than one or the other. In an interview with Barna (see p. 50), family therapist and former pastor Jim Hawkins contends that close, authentic relationships are both preventive medicine and restorative antidote for a host of emotional wounds and mental illness, including depression and addiction. So, as a practical matter, it's all but irrelevant whether being high risk or lacking deep friendships is the causative factor. The point is, pastors need friends.

CLOSE RELATIONSHIPS ARE BOTH PREVENTIVE MEDICINE AND RESTORATIVE ANTIDOTE FOR A HOST OF EMOTIONAL WOUNDS AND MENTAL ILLNESS

7. MONEY

How do pastors see their financial situation?

Average annual income has risen for U.S. pastors by more than 22 percent since 1992, from $53,419 (adjusted for inflation) to $63,314. (For comparison, median personal income in 2015 for U.S. adults over 25 with a bachelor's degree or higher was $71,221.[10]) But while more pastors are earning a salary roughly in line with the national average, how confident do they feel about their financial resilience?

Barna research partner Thrivent Financial developed what it calls the "5S question," an assessment of a person's perceptions of their financial situation. It is not an inventory of a person's *actual* financial situation, but instead reveals their emotions surrounding money and security. People with incomes far above average may report feeling they struggle to meet their expenses, while those with lower incomes may feel secure—and vice versa.

The question is a self-assessment: *Which of the following best describes your current financial situation?*

- **Surviving:** I require financial assistance to get by.
- **Struggling:** I am struggling to keep up with day-to-day expenses.
- **Stable:** I am fairly stable, but just making ends meet.
- **Secure:** I am fairly secure, able to make ends meet and have some left over.
- **Surplus:** I have more than I need for myself and my family.

In research sponsored by Thrivent, Barna surveyed church planters about the state of their finances—a study that included the 5S question—and published the results in the report *Church*

> MOST PASTORS PERCEIVE THEMSELVES TO BE IN BETTER FINANCIAL SHAPE COMPARED TO CHURCH PLANTERS AND U.S. ADULTS OVERALL

Startups and Money.[11] Barna and Pepperdine also included the 5S question in the national study of senior pastors.

The good news is most pastors perceive themselves to be in better financial shape compared to church startup leaders and U.S. adults overall.

PASTORS' PERCEPTIONS OF THEIR FINANCIAL SITUATION, VS. CHURCH PLANTERS & ALL U.S. ADULTS

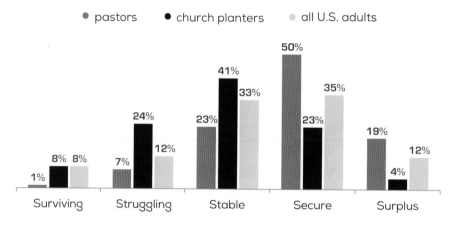

● pastors ● church planters ○ all U.S. adults

	Surviving	Struggling	Stable	Secure	Surplus
pastors	1%	7%	23%	50%	19%
church planters	8%	24%	41%	23%	4%
all U.S. adults	8%	12%	33%	35%	12%

n=374 U.S. Protestant pastors; n=769 U.S. church planters; n=85,000 U.S. adults.

Eleven percent of pastors in the survey report annual compensation of $40,000 or less, and these pastors are more likely than higher-paid colleagues to say they are surviving or struggling, and less likely to think of themselves as having surplus. Pastors of smaller churches and of churches with annual budgets under $100,000 are also more prone to say they are surviving or struggling. So, for many pastors, lower income and smaller ministry budgets correlate to feelings of financial insecurity.

For others, however, financial uncertainty is more closely related to discontent with their ministry: Pastors who express lower levels of satisfaction with their vocation or with their current position are more likely to see themselves as struggling or merely stable and less likely to say they have a surplus of financial resources.

PERCEPTIONS OF FINANCIAL SITUATION, BY VOCATIONAL / CHURCH SATISFACTION

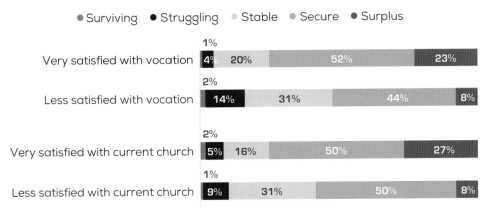

● Surviving   ● Struggling   ● Stable   ● Secure   ● Surplus

Very satisfied with vocation — 1% / 4% / 20% / 52% / 23%

Less satisfied with vocation — 2% / 14% / 31% / 44% / 8%

Very satisfied with current church — 2% / 5% / 16% / 50% / 27%

Less satisfied with current church — 1% / 9% / 31% / 50% / 8%

n=374 U.S. Protestant pastors.

FINANCIAL PREPAREDNESS

In order to understand more thoroughly pastors' perceptions of their financial circumstances, researchers asked them to rate the accuracy of three statements:

- I am confident that I will be financially secure when I retire.
- I am financially prepared for unforeseen expenses, such as a health crisis.
- I have a trustworthy, knowledgeable person to turn to for financial advice.

Overall, seven in 10 pastors say it is completely or somewhat true that they're confident about their retirement security (71%); two-thirds say they are prepared for unexpected expenditures (64%); and three-quarters have a trusted advisor from whom they can get reliable financial guidance (76%). Similar to their answers on the 5S question, however, pastors who earn a lower annual income are less confident in their financial preparedness, while those with higher incomes tend to feel more secure.

PERCEPTIONS OF FINANCIAL PREPAREDNESS, BY INCOME LEVEL
% "completely" + "somewhat true"

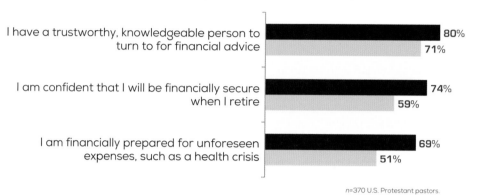

● More than $60K / year   ● Less than $40K / year

I have a trustworthy, knowledgeable person to turn to for financial advice
- **80%**
- **71%**

I am confident that I will be financially secure when I retire
- **74%**
- **59%**

I am financially prepared for unforeseen expenses, such as a health crisis
- **69%**
- **51%**

n=370 U.S. Protestant pastors.

ON QUESTIONS RELATED TO FINANCES, IT'S CLEAR THAT FEWER RESOURCES ARE NO GUARANTEE OF A WORRY-FREE LIFE OR MINISTRY

Lower-income pastors report higher levels of satisfaction at home and in their friendships, and tend to rate their spiritual and mental / emotional well-being more highly than colleagues who earn a higher income. Yet on questions related to finances, it's clear that fewer resources are no guarantee of a worry-free life or ministry.

In addition, confidence related to personal finances appears to affect spiritual leaders' overall contentment and well-being—so helping them deal well with money matters is one way the faith community can help them thrive in ministry.

8. DISORDER

How do pastors cope with mental illness or addiction?

Nearly half of pastors report struggling with depression at some point during their tenure in ministry (46%). A smaller but still significant proportion, about one in five, says they have struggled with an addiction (19%).*

DEPRESSED LEADERS

Depression correlates to several factors. First, lower vocational and ministry satisfaction are related to depression. Pastors who are not very satisfied with their work are nearly twice as likely as those who report the highest level of satisfaction to say depression is or has been a part of their lives (69% vs. 37%). Likewise, those who are not very satisfied with ministry at their current church are more likely than the very satisfied contingent to report depression (54% vs. 40%).

Second, smaller church size and declining attendance correlate to reports of pastoral depression. Roughly half of pastors who lead churches of fewer than 100 (51%) or between 100 to 250 people (56%) have experienced depression, compared to one-third of large-church leaders (32%). Pastors who report declining attendance numbers are also more likely to say they are or have been depressed (62%).

ADDICTED LEADERS

Among the one in five pastors who reports struggling with an addiction, the most common is "porn / sexual addiction" (61%). According to *The Porn Phenomenon*, Barna's study on the ubiquity of pornographic content and widespread porn use, conducted in partnership with Josh McDowell Ministry, 14 percent of all

AMONG THE ONE IN FIVE PASTORS WHO REPORTS STRUGGLING WITH AN ADDICTION, THE MOST COMMON IS TO PORNOGRAPHY

---

* Keep in mind these numbers are self-reports, not clinical assessments.

senior pastors say porn use is a current struggle, and 43 percent say it was a struggle in the past. More than half report they know someone else in ministry who is struggling with porn use (53%).[12]

Generally speaking, the younger the pastor, the more likely he or she is to report an addiction of some kind. And addiction is more common among male than female clergy; this makes sense, given that porn seems to be the most significant issue here, and women are generally less likely than men to seek out porn.[13]

Among those who report an addiction, one in six reports he or she has not sought treatment or recovery (18%). The majority has sought help from one or more sources (82%), most commonly an accountability partner or group (60%), adopting spiritual disciplines or practices (51%) and counseling (25%). Fewer have engaged with a 12-step program (7%) or Celebrate Recovery (6%).

Researchers asked pastors who report an addiction about the impact of disclosure on their ministry, and the split is about even between those who say their decision to be honest has had a positive impact (41%) and those who fear disclosure would have a negative impact (46%). While addiction doesn't appear to be more common than average among those who rate high on Barna's metric of burnout risk, fear of disclosure is much more common. It's unclear whether fear or the risk of burnout is the dominant factor in the correlation—that is, whether high burnout risk leads to fear of disclosure, or fear increases one's burnout risk. Either way, there is a small but significant subset of pastors whose high stress levels are likely compounded by their isolated struggle with addiction.

MENTAL ILLNESS ≠ AN END TO MINISTRY

In more positive news, mental illness appears to be less likely than either burnout or moral failure to end a pastor's ministry. Researchers asked pastors how many senior church leaders they personally know who left pastoral ministry in the past five years "because of a mental illness such as depression, anxiety

MORE THAN HALF OF PASTORS SAY THEY KNOW SOMEONE ELSE IN MINISTRY WHO IS STRUGGLING WITH PORN USE or addiction." One in four says they know just one (25%) and 16 percent report knowing two or more pastors who left ministry for mental health reasons. That combined 41 percent is significantly less than the three-quarters who know at least one pastor who burned out of ministry (76%) and the half who know at least one who left due to moral failure (53%).

Mental and emotional disorders—especially depression—are a common experience among today's pastors. Far from being a ministry-ender, however, it's entirely possible that dealing well (and maybe even openly) with mental health issues when they arise can form a pastor into a wiser and more compassionate shepherd for the people under his or her care.

DEALING WELL WITH MENTAL HEALTH ISSUES WHEN THEY ARISE CAN FORM A PASTOR INTO A WISER AND MORE COMPASSIONATE SHEPHERD

Q&A WITH JIM HAWKINS

JIM HAWKINS

Jim Hawkins entered pastoral ministry in 1976, serving in the United States and in East Africa. In 2010 he was licensed in Indiana as a marriage and family therapist. He is now in private practice at the Christian Counseling Center of Madison County in Anderson, Indiana. One of his specialties is providing counseling and pastoral care for pastors and missionaries and their families. Jim has been married for 43 years to MaryAnn; they have two adult children and four grandchildren.

Q: You became a marriage and family therapist after more than 30 years as a pastor. What have you learned as a counselor that has helped you make sense of the depression you experienced during your pastoral ministry?

A: First, we tend to think of depression as a feeling. But really, most of the time depression is a lack of feeling, or a resistance to a deep experience of grief, anger, pain, disappointment or other dark emotions. It's an *absence* of feeling. The problem is that positive emotions like joy, peace and the sense of connectedness we call love all come from the same part of the brain as negative emotions. When we avoid feeling the dark stuff, we cut ourselves off from emotions that bring light to our lives, including the feelings of transcendence and communion that are our inward experience of God. So, recovering from depression is not about convincing ourselves to feel better, but rather learning to "feel all the feels," as they say on the Internet.

Second, when we're depressed we want to be alone, which is about the worst thing we can do. We think, *I'm bad company. I'm too tired. I don't have the energy to be around people.* But, as I know from personal experience, withdrawing exacerbates the loneliness, emptiness and hopelessness that are at the core of depression. If we want to heal, solitude is counterproductive. Relationships are the lifeline that keeps us from getting sucked down the drain of despair.

Third, understanding the genetic component of mental illness has been incredibly helpful. I was born predisposed to depression, thanks to my parents and their parents before them. I came by it honestly! And learning that freed me from feeling I was to blame for a character flaw called "depression," lifting the burden of shame so the real work could begin. Freedom from shame releases us to do the hard, good work of healing.

Q: Are there features of church ministry that make mental illness a unique challenge for pastors?

A: Two things come to mind. I was born in 1953 into a pastor's home and from early on I understood that pastors aren't supposed to make close friends with anyone in the congregation—because pastors, like parents, can't play favorites.

When I began my own ministry in 1976, this assumption was so ingrained that I didn't even know it existed. But it didn't take long before I had plenty of opportunities to reevaluate—and I concluded it's ridiculous. God created us for relationships. Our minds and emotions are healthiest when we maintain strong attachments to people with whom we can be open, honest and vulnerable. That's not playing favorites. That's being fully alive.

The second thing is this longstanding, theologically distorted idea that if you just pray more, or get in the Word more, you can magically heal your emotional wounds. There is still, even to this day, spiritual stigma attached to mental illness, as though psychological pain is a symptom of spiritual failure. Yet our history is littered with saints who struggled with emotional darkness. Mother Teresa. Saint John of the Cross. The prophet Jeremiah. The writers of the Imprecatory Psalms had anger issues, yet their rage is part of our Holy Scriptures.

We can only go as deep into communion with God as we are willing to uncover, experience and surrender the darker emotions that come with being human. If ministry is standing in the way of that, it has become an obstacle between God and the person called to lead God's people—and obviously that's not God's intention for the Church. We have to find a different way to do ministry.

Q: How would you like to see the church change to be a place where honesty really is the best policy?

A: Through my counseling degree program, I became uneasy with the church's generally accepted definition of addiction as a moral failure. Addiction—whether to a substance or a behavior—is a misguided attempt at self-healing. The absence of secure, reliable relational attachments leaves a person feeling just . . . crappy. (Can I say that?) And compulsive behaviors like using porn, drinking heavily, overeating, cutting, whatever it is, are an effort to not feel so terrible—or, in the case of those whose emotions have shut down completely, an effort to feel *anything*. This understanding of addiction is the reason I'm such a supporter of 12-step programs. I think real and lasting recovery is about relationships—that is, attachments—that a person can form in a good 12-step group.

Why on earth isn't this how we do church? The family of God should be the place where we can expect to find people like us—honest about our brokenness, hopeful for restoration—who trust the communion of saints and the fellowship of the Holy Spirit even on our darkest days. If we can find a way to do church like that, pastors will be first in line.

9. HUMILITY

Are pastors humble enough to change their minds?

Partnering with Pepperdine University gave Barna access to world-class academic researchers whose expertise opened avenues of inquiry we might not otherwise have pursued. Chief among these researchers is Associate Professor of Psychology Elizabeth Krumrei Mancuso, who has developed and validated the Comprehensive Intellectual Humility Scale with a grant from the John Templeton Foundation and Fuller Seminary.[14]

Dr. Krumrei Mancuso and her colleague Steve Rouse define intellectual humility *as a nonthreatening awareness of one's intellectual fallibility that offers a healthy independence of one's intellect from one's ego.* Those who are humble in this way are not threatened by intellectual disagreements, are not overconfident in their knowledge, have respect for others' viewpoints and are open to revising their own views. After learning about her research on this topic, the Barna team was keen to include items from the Comprehensive Intellectual Humility Scale in the national study of Protestant pastors. The agree / disagree question series for the scale includes the following statements:

1. I tend to feel threatened when others disagree with me on topics that are close to my heart.
2. I'm willing to change my mind once it's made up about an important topic.
3. I am willing to hear others out, even if I disagree with them.
4. I welcome different ways of thinking about important topics.
5. My ideas are usually better than other people's ideas.
6. When I am really confident in a belief, there is very little chance that belief is wrong.

SPECIAL REPORT

by Elizabeth Krumrei Mancuso

ELIZABETH KRUMREI MANCUSO

Elizabeth Krumrei Mancuso holds a PhD in Clinical Psychology and is Associate Professor of Psychology at Pepperdine University. She has published work in the areas of virtues (intellectual humility, gratitude, forgiveness), religion, spirituality, stress, coping, mental health and prostitution, and is coauthor of *Faith from a Positive Psychology Perspective*. Elizabeth has provided psychotherapy at mental health centers for adults and children, and currently teaches courses in psychotherapy, family therapy, advanced research methodology and psychology of religion.

Leadership typically involves some form of power differential in which a leader has greater influence than the people they lead. This is true in religious contexts as well, where the perspectives of faith leaders often come to carry more weight than that of their congregants. Perhaps this is why the apostle James wrote that teachers would be judged more strictly (see Jas. 3:1). For these reasons, intellectual humility is important for faith leaders.

The Barna survey of Protestant faith leaders included six items from the Comprehensive Intellectual Humility Scale. Pastors express high levels of respect for others' viewpoints, with more than nine out of 10 agreeing that they welcome different ways of thinking about important topics (92%) and that they are willing to hear others out, even if they disagree (99%; although percentages are high across the board, welcoming diverse ways of thinking is most strongly endorsed by pastors of larger churches and those who have attended seminary). A substantial majority also indicates they are willing to change their minds once they are made up about an important topic (84%), which is another sign of intellectual humility.

On the other hand, many pastors seem to struggle with overconfidence. Seven in 10 leaders say that, when they are really confident in a belief, there is very little chance that belief is wrong (69%). This may indicate that faith leaders don't readily recognize the

MORE THAN NINE
OUT OF 10 PASTORS
SAY THEY WELCOME
DIFFERENT WAYS
OF THINKING ABOUT
IMPORTANT TOPICS

intellectual biases to which all humans are prone. Research has shown a weak-to-nonexistent relationship between confidence in one's beliefs and the accuracy of those beliefs.[15] Being intellectually humble involves appreciating the tentative nature of knowledge, regardless of one's level of confidence. Interestingly, this is the only humility item with a gender difference: Men (72%) are much more likely than women (39%) to agree there is little chance they are wrong when they are very confident in a belief.

Three in 10 pastors believes their ideas are usually better than other people's (30%), which could be another indication of intellectual overconfidence. On the other hand, it's possible this assessment reflects accurate self-knowledge; pastors who have been in ministry for more than 15 years (32%) are more likely than pastors with shorter ministry tenure (21%) to believe their ideas tend to be better than other people's. There may be something about greater ministry experience that puts pastors in a position to have better ideas than the people around them—or, conversely, more ministry experience may be associated with becoming overconfident about one's ideas.

Another three in 10 pastors says they tend to feel threatened when others disagree with them on a topic close to their heart (29%). This indicates that some leaders struggle to separate their intellect from their ego; they feel as though it is a personal attack when others express differing opinions. With age and experience, however, this struggle seems to decline; fewer Elder pastors (16%) than Gen-X (29%) and Boomer (30%) leaders report feeling threatened by intellectual disagreements; and pastors who have been in ministry 30 years or more (24%) feel significantly less threatened by intellectual disagreements than pastors who have been in ministry less than 15 years (34%).

Taken together, these findings indicate that church leaders today seem to possess great strengths yet also face some challenges when it comes to intellectual humility. Their respect for others' viewpoints and willingness to revise their own views when warranted are qualities that can lead to successful interactions with other religious leaders and with congregants, such as in the context of making decisions in the faith community and providing pastoral care. At the same time, a substantial proportion of pastors may be blinded by intellectual overconfidence or may experience intellectual disagreement as a personal threat. If this occurs, pastors could lack awareness of errors in their thinking, overlook opportunities to learn from others' ideas and knowledge, and respond defensively when people offer differing perspectives.

In addition to potential links to successful ministry, intellectual humility appears to correlate to pastors' satisfaction with their vocation. Those with higher levels of intellectual humility report greater vocational satisfaction than those with lower levels. Specifically, pastors who feel threatened when others disagree with them and who are less willing to change their minds express less satisfaction with their vocation than those who experience less threat in the face of disagreement and who are more willing to change their minds.

It's important to note that intellectual humility does not involve abandoning truth claims. In fact, this kind of humility appears to be unrelated to constructs such as conformity, social confidence and low self-regard, and even shows slight positive associations with higher self-confidence.[16] There is no inherent conflict between faith leaders confidently holding personal beliefs and simultaneously possessing intellectual humility.

Previous research has shown that intellectual humility is associated with a host of beneficial qualities, including perspective taking, empathy, gratitude, altruism, benevolence, less power

> THERE IS NO INHERENT CONFLICT BETWEEN CONFIDENTLY HOLDING PERSONAL BELIEFS AND SIMULTANEOUSLY POSSESSING INTELLECTUAL HUMILITY

seeking and open-mindedness.[17] These qualities are likely to benefit pastors in their efforts to minister to others.

Finally, while pastors have room to improve on a few aspects of intellectual humility, on most items these leaders are on par with or demonstrate somewhat greater humility than U.S. adults overall. "When I am really confident in a belief, there is very little chance that belief is wrong" is an obvious exception; notably, female pastors (39%) are in line with the national norm (44%) on this statement, while male leaders' outsized confidence (72%) skews the average among all pastors.

MEASURES OF INTELLECTUAL HUMILITY: PASTORS VS. ALL U.S. ADULTS

% "strongly" + "somewhat agree" among U.S. pastors and U.S. adults 18 and older

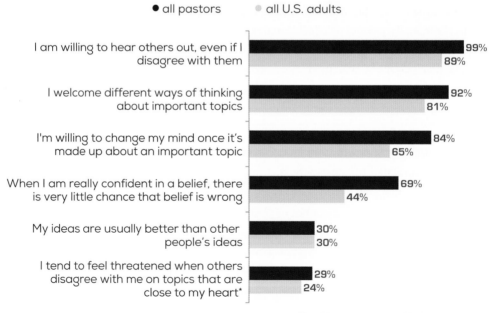

● all pastors ● all U.S. adults

I am willing to hear others out, even if I disagree with them — 99% / 89%

I welcome different ways of thinking about important topics — 92% / 81%

I'm willing to change my mind once it's made up about an important topic — 84% / 65%

When I am really confident in a belief, there is very little chance that belief is wrong — 69% / 44%

My ideas are usually better than other people's ideas — 30% / 30%

I tend to feel threatened when others disagree with me on topics that are close to my heart* — 29% / 24%

n=524 U.S. Protestant pastors; n=1,025 U.S. adults 18 and older.
*The difference between pastors and U.S. adults is not statistically significant for this statement.

10. CALLING
THE AGE OF CALLING

More than half of all U.S. pastors sense a call to ministry between the ages of 14 and 21. Here's a timing breakdown of this pivotal experience.

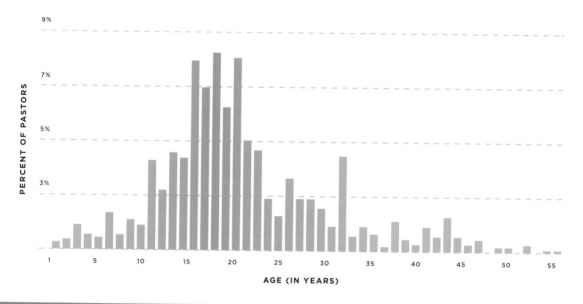

PERCENT OF PASTORS

AGE (IN YEARS)

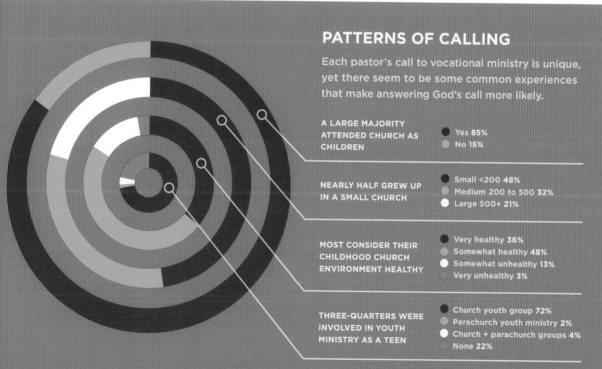

PATTERNS OF CALLING

Each pastor's call to vocational ministry is unique, yet there seem to be some common experiences that make answering God's call more likely.

A LARGE MAJORITY ATTENDED CHURCH AS CHILDREN
- Yes 85%
- No 15%

NEARLY HALF GREW UP IN A SMALL CHURCH
- Small <200 48%
- Medium 200 to 500 32%
- Large 500+ 21%

MOST CONSIDER THEIR CHILDHOOD CHURCH ENVIRONMENT HEALTHY
- Very healthy 36%
- Somewhat healthy 48%
- Somewhat unhealthy 13%
- Very unhealthy 3%

THREE-QUARTERS WERE INVOLVED IN YOUTH MINISTRY AS A TEEN
- Church youth group 72%
- Parachurch youth ministry 2%
- Church + parachurch groups 4%
- None 22%

Are pastors confident in their call to ministry?

A majority of pastors says they felt their call to ministry between the ages of 14 and 21 (53%)—but do they still feel it? How confident are church leaders in their calling from God to shepherd his people?

Very confident, in large measure. Three in 10 report they are "just as confident" today as when they first entered pastoral ministry (31%), and two-thirds say they are even "more confident" now than then (66%). Just 3 percent admit they are "less confident," and these leaders tend to be younger, part of a mainline denomination or, most often, leading a church with declining attendance.

A pastor's confidence in his or her calling is correlated to how satisfied they are with their work and with their current church ministry. Pastors who are very satisfied in one or both areas are apt to express increased assurance, while those who are less satisfied tend also to be less confident.

While confidence in pastoral calling remains robust overall, roughly six in 10 pastors (58%) say they have felt "inadequate for [their] ministry or calling" during the past three months, either frequently (12%) or sometimes (45%). Leaders of churches with declining attendance feel this inadequacy most acutely.

Researchers examined the relationship of confidence in one's calling with feelings of ministry inadequacy and of being "energized by ministry work." As one might expect, the small percentage of pastors who feel less confident in their calling today than when they started their ministry do not feel energized by ministry work as often as those who are more confident. Similarly, leaders who are less confident today in their call to ministry feel inadequate for their calling much more frequently than those who are just as or more confident than when they began.

These data suggest the importance of regular reflection on one's motivation for engaging in ministry. As Simon Sinek famously advises, leaders should "start with why."[18] Confidence that God has called you to your work appears to be a buttress against inevitable challenges that arise, so consider how to tend and grow reliance on the God who called you—and how to bolster that confidence in the lives and hearts of other pastors you know well.

CONFIDENCE IN MINISTRY CALLING TODAY COMPARED TO WHEN PASTORS BEGAN THEIR MINISTRY

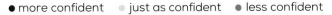

● more confident   ● just as confident   ● less confident

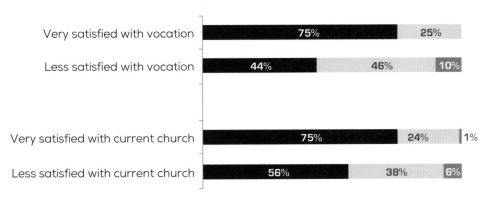

	more confident	just as confident	less confident
Very satisfied with vocation	75%	25%	
Less satisfied with vocation	44%	46%	10%
Very satisfied with current church	75%	24%	1%
Less satisfied with current church	56%	38%	6%

n=900 U.S. Protestant pastors.

PART II
CHURCH LEADERSHIP

CHURCH LEADERSHIP

Pastors are called by God to lead a local church to be Christ's body and continue his mission of redemption and reconciliation. And most keep at it because no other career or vocation could come close to the fulfillment they experience by answering their call to ministry.

Part II explores pastors' thoughts on leading a church. How well are they equipped for ministry? With whom do they lead—and how is it working? What is it like to lead a church? How do they interact with people inside and outside the church? In what ways is pastoring different for women? How are pastors engaging with the next generation of church leaders? How important are denominations and other area congregations to their church's ministry? What part of their job do they enjoy most and what frustrates them most about church ministry? And how well do their day-to-day tasks fit with their calling and gifts?

By and large, pastors report greater satisfaction than frustration, and a sense that their pastoral duties are well-matched to their skills and sense of call—but the handful who paint a less rosy picture of their ministry experience are not sure where to go from here. Perhaps by better understanding their experiences, the Church can help.

73% Church leaders are educated and (usually) well-prepared.

Three-quarters have pursued higher education—most commonly a bachelor's degree or M. Div.—and feel it was good training. Seminary, however, gets mixed reviews.

Pastors are out in front, but not alone.

60% of leaders are primarily responsible for their church's vision and direction, but 80% work with a board of elders or similar team—and most are "hugely supportive" of the pastor.

The neglect of prayer within leader teams is a red flag.

Troublingly, just one-third of pastors engage in "frequent prayer together" with their elders.

In-person communication with congregants is valued and valuable.

Even in a digital age, church members most often offer feedback face to face, whether in public or private. On the whole, pastors say these discussions are encouraging and helpful.

9% Ministry opportunities for women are increasing, but challenging.

Women now represent 9% of senior pastors—triple the percentage of 25 years ago—bug they frequently lead smaller churches and feel greater scrutiny.

Pastors love being in the pulpit.

When listing their strengths, pastors name preaching, Bible knowledge and practical theology. Teaching is not only the center of Sunday morning, but also their favorite task.

People problems are the chief source of frustration.

Leaders identify churchgoers' lack of commitment and spiritual maturity as their top frustrations, surpassing even administrative burdens and church politics.

Denominations are important, but not typically influential.

Half of church leaders say their affiliation is very strong, but just one-quarter says their denomination has a lot of influence on their ministry activities.

7 OUT OF 10 Pastors worry about finding future leaders.

Most would encourage a young person to pursue ministry as a career, but 7 out of 10 think it's becoming more difficult to identify promising pastoral candidates.

Low-risk leaders feel their primary tasks "fit" their calling.

Most pastors at low risk of burnout and spiritual problems say their day-to-day tasks are a good match with their calling and giftedness.

11. PREPARATION
TRAINING PASTORS

Pursuing higher education remains a popular choice for pastors. Here's a close study of the academic experiences of today's ministers.

WHERE PASTORS STUDY

COLLEGE / UNIVERSITY	73%
SEMINARY / SCHOOL OF THEOLOGY	45%
COMMUNITY COLLEGE	4%
OTHER	4%
TRADE SCHOOL	2%
DID NOT ATTEND	2%

The most common degrees among pastors include a Bachelor of Arts / Science (70%) and a Master of Divinity (49%).

One out of five pastors (21%) has received a doctoral degree of some kind, most often a DMin (14%).

FIRST-CAREER DEGREES

A significant number of today's pastors didn't start out that way. Here are some of the degrees they earned before becoming "second-career clergy."

Juris Doctor

Botany

Physical Therapy

Public and International Affairs

Music Education

DEGREES OF PREPARATION

Nearly three-quarters of pastors rate their ministry training as excellent or good.

72%

When it comes to how well seminary prepares people for effective church leadership, pastors offer mixed reviews.

8%	very well
50%	somewhat well
34%	not too well
8%	not at all well

The top three things pastors wish they had been better prepared for:

 29% counseling burdens or solving people's problems

 29% administrative burdens

 27% handling conflict

Pastors at high risk of burnout are more likely to feel underprepared in all aspects of ministry, particularly relational responsibilities.

50% handling conflict

38% administrative burdens

37% the importance of delegation and training people

34% church politics

34% challenges in leadership

Some factors feel especially challenging for specific segments of pastors.

Pastors under 50:

34%
administrative burdens

9%
that ministry "never gets easier"

Female pastors:

18%
high expectations

15%
the sense that they "must do everything"

Seminary attendees:

36%
handling conflict

24%
church politics

Pastors in churches with high annual budgets ($1M+):

39%
the importance of delegation and training people

28%
challenges in leadership

n=824 U.S. Protestant pastors.

How well are pastors equipped for their ministry?

One set of goals for *The State of Pastors* was to understand how people who receive a call to ministry go on to prepare for their vocation. This includes documenting education levels among pastors and assessing the degree to which they believe their education has effectively equipped them for ministry. As a category of workers, pastors are well-educated—but the range of educational attainment runs the gamut.

For a majority of pastors, formal education is a key component of ministry preparation. Three-quarters of pastors in the study attended a Bible college (22%) or a college or university (51%), and seven in 10 earned at least a baccalaureate degree (70%). A majority also went on to graduate education of some kind, whether a Master of Divinity (49%) or some other master's-level program (31%), and one in five received a doctorate (21%), most often a Doctor of Ministry (14%).

Most pastors attended an educational institution affiliated with their denomination (69%). Having done so is more common among pastors under 50 years of age than those 50 and older, and more common among white pastors than leaders of color. Although pastors of churches with more than 1,000 weekend attenders are a small subgroup, it's interesting to note they are less likely than the norm to have attended a denomination-affiliated college or university (49% vs. 69%).

Many educational institutions are actively involved in placing graduates in church ministry positions, and two out of three pastors who attended such a school say their alma mater was at least somewhat helpful in this regard (65%). However, only 35 percent gave their school the highest marks in this regard, suggesting room for growth in placement programs for those who have earned a degree.

Advanced education appears to be more important in mainline denominations than in non-mainline churches; one reason is that it's more common for mainline denominations to require a seminary degree before one may be considered for ordination. Mainline pastors are more likely than their non-mainline peers to have attended a college or university (67% vs. 46%) versus a Bible college (4% vs. 28%), and to have attended seminary (62% vs. 40%). They are also more apt to have earned a Master of Divinity (83% vs. 37%) or a Doctor of Ministry (22% vs. 11%).

Pastors offer mixed reviews when it comes to how well seminary prepares people to be effective church leaders: Only 9 percent of pastors give top marks, saying seminary does "very well"; half say it does "somewhat well." Two in five pastors believe seminary does "not too well" (34%) or "not at all well" (8%) at preparing people for effective church leadership.

Whether a pastor attends seminary seems to bias him or her toward or against its practical value. That is, pastors who attended seminary are twice as likely as those who did not attend to say such institutions are doing very well at preparing people to effectively lead churches today. And those who did not attend are twice as likely as those who did to say seminaries are doing not at all well when it comes to preparing pastors for ministry.

PREPARATION GAPS

Researchers asked all pastors—seminarians and non-seminarians—to identify areas of ministry for which they wish they'd been better prepared. "Counseling / people problems to solve," the "administrative burden" and "handling conflict" come in at a statistical tie. These are followed by "balancing ministry and administration," "delegating / training people" and "challenges in leadership," also in a virtual tie. Clearly, many pastors feel they were not adequately prepared for leading people, dealing with conflict and the administrative tasks that are part and parcel of pastoring in the 21st century.

Additional areas of inadequate preparation are shown in the chart. Keep in mind that, given the total size of today's

AREAS OF MINISTRY FOR WHICH PASTORS WISH THEY HAD BEEN BETTER PREPARED

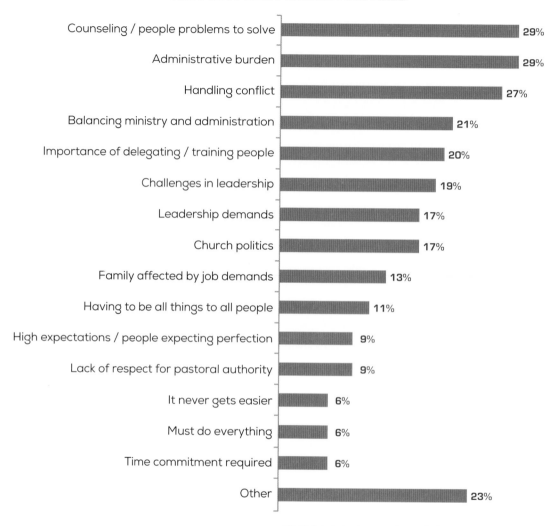

Counseling / people problems to solve	29%
Administrative burden	29%
Handling conflict	27%
Balancing ministry and administration	21%
Importance of delegating / training people	20%
Challenges in leadership	19%
Leadership demands	17%
Church politics	17%
Family affected by job demands	13%
Having to be all things to all people	11%
High expectations / people expecting perfection	9%
Lack of respect for pastoral authority	9%
It never gets easier	6%
Must do everything	6%
Time commitment required	6%
Other	23%

n=824 U.S. Protestant pastors; respondents could select all that apply.

church-leader population, even small percentages reflect potentially substantial gaps in the preparation pastors are receiving.

Church size plays a role in what sort of preparation a pastor wishes they had received. For their part, pastors of large churches (250-plus weekend attenders) are much more likely than their

colleagues who lead small (less than 100) and midsize congregations (100 to 250) to say they wish they'd been better prepared to
delegate and train people. (Given that they're dealing with larger
staffs and a bigger pool of potential ministry volunteers, this difference makes sense.) It's a similar story with handling conflict:
One-third who lead large churches say they would like to have
had better preparation in this regard, compared to one in four
small and midsize church leaders.

MANY PASTORS FEEL THEY
WERE NOT ADEQUATELY
PREPARED FOR LEADING
PEOPLE, DEALING WITH
CONFLICT AND DOING
ADMINISTRATIVE TASKS

DESIRE FOR BETTER PREPARATION, BY CHURCH SIZE

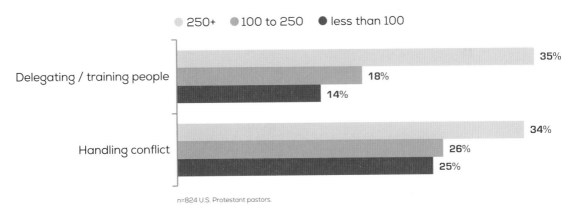

● 250+ ● 100 to 250 ● less than 100

Delegating / training people — 35% / 18% / 14%

Handling conflict — 34% / 26% / 25%

n=824 U.S. Protestant pastors.

Not surprisingly, pastors who rate high on the burnout risk
metric also wish they'd been better prepared for handling conflict
(50%) and for "church politics" (34%)—so it's not a surprise that
fewer than half of these leader rate their overall ministry preparation training as excellent (15%) or at least good (29%), compared to seven in 10 among all pastors (24% excellent, 48% good).

The data confirm that education matters to pastors. Equally
apparent is that most church leaders feel unprepared to minister
as effectively in a changing context as they would like. In order
to meet the needs of leaders in today's complex times, our institutions—Bible colleges and seminaries, denominations and li-
censing organizations—must continue to reevaluate and rethink
ministry preparation models and pastoral pedagogy.

12. GOVERNANCE

With whom do pastors lead their church— and is it working?

Researchers also delved into an area of leadership that can make or break a congregation: governance. Most pastors say they are primarily responsible for setting the vision and direction of the church (60%) or are part of a team that develops the vision and direction together (35%). Regardless, most senior leaders do not lead alone. A majority reports to a board of elders or similar group of laypeople (such as deacons, etc., 80%); this is slightly more true in mainline churches, where nearly nine out of 10 pastors work with a board (88%), compared to three-quarters of non-mainline pastors (77%). It's also more common for mainline pastors to be part of a visioning-directing team rather than solely responsible; the opposite is true for non-mainline leaders.

Most pastors express positive perceptions of the elders-pastor relationship, although there is range of attitudes they hold toward this governing body. At the most positive end of the scale, a majority of pastors says their board is "hugely supportive" of them as a pastor (67%), describes the relationship as generating "healthy accountability" (60%) and indicates they have "clear and shared vision and values" (57%). However, there are signs of possible weakness between pastors and elders. Pastors less commonly categorize the relationship as "a powerful partnership" (44%) or say they engage in "frequent prayer together" (34%).

Positive pastor-elders relationships are most often found in large congregations. In fact, pastors of 250 or more adults are twice as likely as leaders in smaller churches to say their relationship with elders is a powerful partnership (64% vs. 34%). By its nature, survey research does not reveal causation but only helps us uncover correlations. Yet the correlation here may suggest smaller

POSITIVE PASTOR-ELDERS DYNAMIC, BY CHURCH SIZE

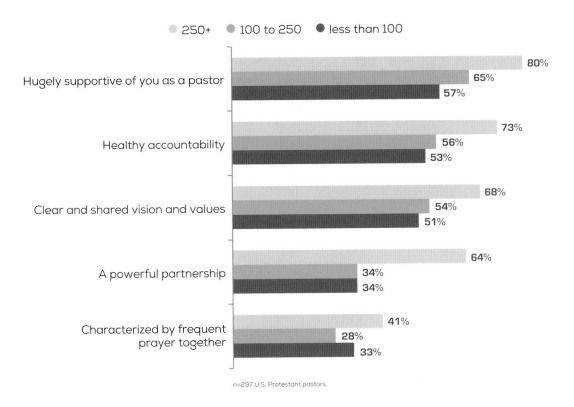

● 250+ ● 100 to 250 ● less than 100

Hugely supportive of you as a pastor
80%
65%
57%

Healthy accountability
73%
56%
53%

Clear and shared vision and values
68%
54%
51%

A powerful partnership
64%
34%
34%

Characterized by frequent prayer together
41%
28%
33%

n=297 U.S. Protestant pastors.

churches stay small in part because laypeople lack a strong sense of partnership with the senior pastor. Reinforcing this possibility, those who lead growing churches are also more likely than leaders of shrinking congregations to feel their pastor-elders relationship is a powerful partnership (52% vs. 36%). Church expansion may depend at least in part on the support a pastor receives from the elders, the clarity of their shared vision and values and the power of their partnership to lead the church's mission.

Perhaps one of the most significant red flags revealed by the findings is how infrequently pastors and elders pray together. In research Barna conducted in Scotland, researchers discovered that growing churches *pray missionally and make prayer a mission*. One way growing Scottish churches differentiate themselves

CHURCH EXPANSION MAY DEPEND AT LEAST IN PART ON THE SUPPORT A PASTOR RECEIVES FROM THE ELDERS AND THE POWER OF THEIR PARTNERSHIP

NEGATIVE PASTOR-ELDERS DYNAMIC, BY BURNOUT RISK

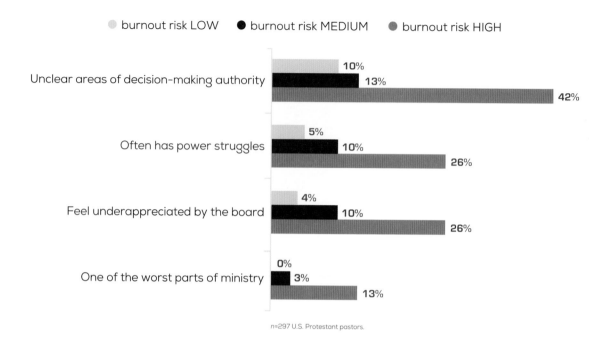

● burnout risk LOW　　● burnout risk MEDIUM　　● burnout risk HIGH

Unclear areas of decision-making authority
- 10%
- 13%
- 42%

Often has power struggles
- 5%
- 10%
- 26%

Feel underappreciated by the board
- 4%
- 10%
- 26%

One of the worst parts of ministry
- 0%
- 3%
- 13%

n=297 U.S. Protestant pastors.

from flat or declining congregations is by praying "specifically for the challenges of living faithfully in a post-Christian culture."[19] This finding requires an obvious follow-up question: How can pastors strengthen the practice of spiritual disciplines, such as prayer, in the teams with whom they lead?

The research also uncovered significant correlations between a positive pastor-elders relationship and both longer ministry tenure and higher levels of ministry satisfaction. Pastors who are satisfied with their current church ministry tend to report a more positive relationship with their governing board than those who are less satisfied. Conversely, discontented leaders are more apt than the norm to describe the relationship in negative terms. There are "unclear areas of decision-making authority" (42% vs. 18% all pastors). They often have "power struggles" (39% vs. 12%). They "feel underappreciated by the board" (36% vs. 11%). One in five would go so far as to say the pastor-elders dynamic is "one of the worst parts of ministry" (19% vs. 4%).

A parallel trend is at work among pastors who are at high risk of burnout, suggesting a connection not only between a healthy leadership team and a growing church, but also between a healthy leadership team and a healthy pastor.

Again, it is not possible to pinpoint the direction of causation— that is, whether the negative relationship contributes to the pastor's risk of burnout or the pastor's stress-related problems contribute to a strained pastor-elders dynamic. But either way, there is a strong correlation between high risk of burnout and relational challenges within the church's leadership.

All these data indicate that a strong, mutually supportive relationship between a pastor and the governing team is integral to church health and to the pastor's health. Relational harmony in this area lowers a leader's risk of burning out and lengthens his or her tenure in ministry.

A STRONG, MUTUALLY SUPPORTIVE RELATIONSHIP BETWEEN A PASTOR AND THE GOVERNING TEAM IS INTEGRAL TO CHURCH HEALTH AND TO THE PASTOR'S HEALTH

13. LEADING

What is it like to pastor a church?

Shepherding a church is its own unique experience, in many ways unlike any other job or career. But there are elements of pastoring that resemble other vocations—sometimes for the better, but occasionally for the worse.

Barna asked pastors to think about the tasks and demands of church ministry and then choose which of two job functions most resembles their personal experience of being a pastor. So, for example, pastors could choose between entrepreneur and manager or between referee and doctor. These were set up as forced-choice questions—respondents had to pick one or the other—to help researchers get a clear sense of what pastors are feeling and experiencing in ministry.

Pastors' level of satisfaction with their current church, as well as where they land on the Barna risk metrics, appear to impact their choices. As a rule, pastors who are less satisfied in their current position are more prone to feel like a manager, counselor, referee and administrator, and less like an entrepreneur, coach, doctor and leader. Similar percentages are found among pastors who are high on the metric of burnout risk.

Note the consistency on one side of the ledger: Lower ministry satisfaction is correlated to job functions that react or respond. On the other hand, pastors who select more assertive terms tend to report a more satisfying experience in ministry. Of course, choosing more passive self-descriptors does not automatically set up a pastor for diminished satisfaction! Many pastors are effective managers, counselors and administrators and are quite satisfied with their ministry experiences. Yet many leaders who lack intention and empowerment, or who feel subject to the whims of their congregations, show signs of depleted resilience.

LOWER MINISTRY SATISFACTION IS CORRELATED TO JOB FUNCTIONS THAT REACT OR RESPOND

THE EXPERIENCE OF BEING A PASTOR, BY SATISFACTION WITH CURRENT CHURCH

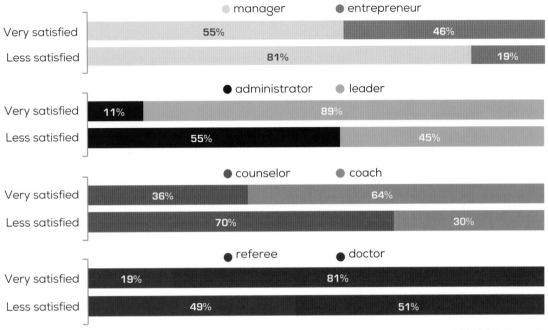

● manager   ● entrepreneur

Very satisfied: 55% / 46%
Less satisfied: 81% / 19%

● administrator   ● leader

Very satisfied: 11% / 89%
Less satisfied: 55% / 45%

● counselor   ● coach

Very satisfied: 36% / 64%
Less satisfied: 70% / 30%

● referee   ● doctor

Very satisfied: 19% / 81%
Less satisfied: 49% / 51%

n=516 U.S. Protestant pastors.

Here's another way to look at it: Pastors who are discontent in their current position seem to spend much of their energy on logistics and operations (manager-administrator) and on helping people work out their relational issues (counselor-referee). This theory is bolstered when we consider the top frustrations of low-satisfaction leaders: "Implementing change in the church" (27%) and "church politics" (38%) are among the top five tasks that cause these pastors frustration—yet these irritations are barely on the radar of very satisfied pastors.

In what ways can your ministry efforts focus on innovation and visioning (entrepreneur-leader) and on equipping people to be spiritually active and healthy (coach-doctor)? If your role involves managing, refereeing and so on, or if you lead people on your team who serve in these capacities, how can you sustain ministry resilience over the long haul?

Q&A WITH SVETLANA PAPAZOV

SVETLANA PAPAZOV

Dr. Svetlana Papazov is a
wife, mother, church planter,
entrepreneur, educator and
executive coach. Pulling from
her diverse experience in small
business, academia and ministry,
she launched Real Life Church, a
marketplace church that integrates
faith and entrepreneurship.
Svetlana is also founder and CEO of
Real Life Center for Entrepreneurial
and Leadership Excellence in
Richmond, Virginia. Her passion
is whole-life discipleship, and she
deeply cares about the holistic
development of communities to
shape world influencers and work
toward culture transformation.

Q: What are leadership skills that you believe translate to all vocations—not just ministry, but any leadership role? Have you found you use the same set of skills or similar approaches in business and ministry?

A: There are two leadership skills that I consider of particular importance to success in business or church: *vision* and *inspired action.*

Before leaders can take their followers into the future, they must envision the future. When an entrepreneur starts a business, they must picture the mature business in full, and then reverse-engineer it. Otherwise, their business is only going to confirm the statistic that 90 percent of small businesses fail in the first five years of being a startup.[20] Vision is also especially important to the pastor and the success of their church. Without a God-breathed, clear vision for the church's DNA—its unique place in the global body of Christ, growth structure and supporting systems—the local church may also find itself becoming a grim statistic.

Just as important as envisioning the future is taking divinely inspired action toward that future. Leaders must sometimes be willing to become unpopular until their model is proven, boldly taking risks as they put structures and systems in place to ensure the success of their venture

Q: What are some basic business skills you think pastors sometimes neglect or do not see as essential to leading a ministry? How can the next generation of pastors receive more well-rounded preparation?

A: A successful business owner asks, "Who is my ideal client?" so that their business can serve that demographic in the best possible way. Pastors may feel awkward asking, "Who is our target audience? Who does our church want to reach?" It feels limiting. But the reality is that if a church takes time to discover where God has positioned them and how their passions address the problems around them, they will have discovered the work that the Holy Spirit has prepared them to do.

Another important business skill for ministry leaders is finding creative revenue streams. Pastors will elevate their churches if they are open to considering innovative ways of achieving sustainability and generating funds, in addition to the congregants' tithes and offerings. What if pastors served their communities better by renting out building space that stays empty most of the week for entrepreneurial training, holiday events, continued education programs, corporate retreats or office use? And what if in doing so they created familiarity with people who other-wise would never step inside their buildings? It is a win-win situation: reaching new demograph-ics *and* generating funds for more missional work. Pastors may feel that strategizing about "making money" taints their mission but, just like a business, a church requires fiscal viability to carry out transformational activities. The next generation of pastors will benefit from taking both leadership and business classes in order to receive more comprehensive preparation to pastor a 21st-century church.

Q: **Why do you believe so strongly in the connection between worship and the workplace?**
A: In my own experience in reaching and serving entrepreneurs, I observe firsthand the growing disconnect between faith and the marketplace, especially among small business owners and the church. Not because entrepreneurs are not looking for spirituality, but because they feel that the church has become irrelevant to them or doesn't understand their struggles. Pastors often shy away from preaching about business and the good that it does for our society. In ad-dition, some business owners remain skeptical of the church, assuming that if pastors reach out to them, they are only interested in their monetary support for the church's projects.

I believe that God is the God of all life, and that his Word reveals the most inspiring model for thriving economies. To separate biblical principles such as creativity, just wages, human dignity and stewardship from the workplace is to set our societies up for failure. Only holistic Christianity that incorporates faith into the *whole* life—uniting work, ministry, worship and family—will succeed in bringing the reality of God's presence to the professional realm. When believers engage vocation as an act of worship to God (see. Col. 3:23–24), they introduce the strongest work ethics into the marketplace. They become modern, Spirit-filled Bezalels (see Ex. 31:1–5) who are noted for their skill and knowledge in all kinds of work, modeling righteous living in their local cultures and pointing their neighbors to hope-filled community in Christ.

14. COMMUNICATION

How do pastors interact with people in their church?

Churchgoers offer feedback to pastors about their ministry or leadership in a variety of ways. Most commonly, according to pastors, congregants give input face to face in private (64%), face to face in public (e.g., after church, 49%) or via email message (44%). Pastors in every age, denomination, ethnic and gender category put these three communication methods in their top three.

There are significant differences, however, when it comes to church size—in particular, leaders of small churches appear to be more accessible than pastors of large churches for personal interactions with their congregants. Pastors of congregations with attendance of 250 or more are twice as likely as small-church leaders of fewer than 100 to say they get an email message, and less likely to report meeting face to face or receiving a personal phone call.

As one might expect, younger pastors are more apt than their elders to get congregants' input through text messages and social media, while phone calls remain a popular mode of communication among older leaders. Female pastors are also more likely than men to receive emails with input from churchgoers, though the reasons for this difference are unclear.

But what about the content of the feedback pastors receive? Is it mostly helpful, encouraging and gracious—or more unhelpful, hurtful and critical?

INPUT FOR PASTORS

On the whole, pastors tend to find the communications they receive from congregants to be encouraging, helpful and affirming. Pastors are split, however, on whether their congregants'

COMMON WAYS CONGREGANTS COMMUNICATE WITH PASTORS, BY CHURCH SIZE

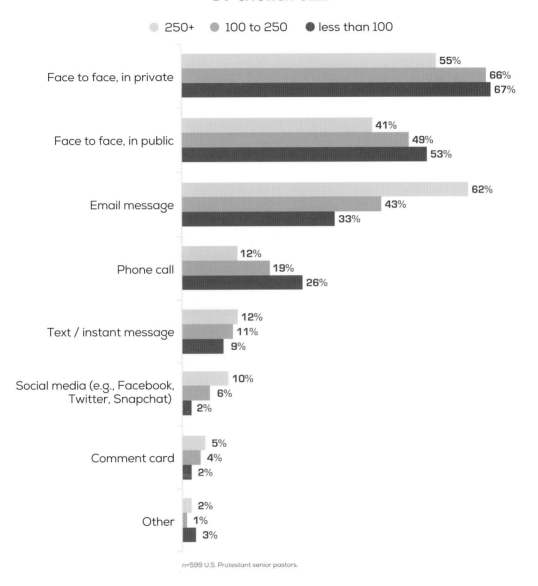

● 250+   ● 100 to 250   ● less than 100

Face to face, in private
- 55%
- 66%
- 67%

Face to face, in public
- 41%
- 49%
- 53%

Email message
- 62%
- 43%
- 33%

Phone call
- 12%
- 19%
- 26%

Text / instant message
- 12%
- 11%
- 9%

Social media (e.g., Facebook, Twitter, Snapchat)
- 10%
- 6%
- 2%

Comment card
- 5%
- 4%
- 2%

Other
- 2%
- 1%
- 3%

n=599 U.S. Protestant senior pastors.

ON THE WHOLE, PASTORS TEND TO FIND CONGREGANTS' COMMUNICATIONS TO BE ENCOURAGING, HELPFUL AND AFFIRMING

communications are generally knowledgeable or uninformed. Overall, women and younger pastors perceive church members' comments about their leadership or ministry as less positive compared to men and older ministers. This is particularly true when it comes to evaluating whether input is gracious or critical, affirming or judging, and helpful or unhelpful. Women are more likely than men to say congregants' comments are judging, critical or unhelpful; the same is true for pastors under 50 compared to those 50 and older.

Similar trends can be seen among pastors of small, midsize and large churches. Generally speaking, pastors of churches of less than 100 in attendance perceive their members' input as less positive compared to leaders of larger churches.

PASTORS' PERCEPTION OF MEMBERS' FEEDBACK, BY GENDER AND AGE					
	% All	% Women	% Men	% Under 50	% 50+
encouraging	83	80	83	80	86
hurtful	10	13	10	13	8
helpful	77	72	79	74	82
unhelpful	15	27	14	19	12
affirming	70	63	70	65	73
judging	17	31	16	21	14
gracious	72	53	74	66	77
critical	22	36	21	29	18
knowledgeable	43	38	43	39	45
uninformed	46	54	45	54	40

It's possible (and even likely) that there are multiple, discrete factors at work here. By virtue of their less frequent personal interactions with their congregants, pastors of larger churches may be insulated somewhat from unhelpful, critical or judgmental encounters. A pastor of a small congregation—who is also more likely to be young, a woman or both—does not have that luxury. It's also possible that members of smaller churches have become accustomed to airing their grievances.

In addition, as we will see in the following chapter, female pastors feel greater pressure than their male colleagues when it comes to people's expectations. Some of this pressure to "do everything" or attain "perfection" may be felt through members' communications; alternately, the existential pressure women pastors experience (see "Women" beginning on p. 82) may predispose them to perceive members' communications as more negative.

Younger pastors' more negative perceptions may be due in part to their preferred modes of communication: Text-based messaging is notorious for being difficult to parse and interpret, especially with regard to the sender's intention and emotional state. It may also be that younger pastors haven't yet developed the "thick skin" that some leaders argue is essential for leaders who want to be in long-term church ministry.[21]

Q&A WITH BOBBY GRUENEWALD

BOBBY GRUENEWALD

Bobby Gruenewald serves as Pastor, Innovation Leader at Life.Church and is the founder of the YouVersion Bible app, which has been installed on 250 million devices. As one of the leading voices in the Church on innovation and the use of technology, Bobby has been featured in *The New York Times*, *TechCrunch*, CNN and more. Prior to joining the Life.Church team in 2001, he started and sold two technology companies and served in advisory capacities for various startups and venture capital funds. He and his wife, Melissa, live in Edmond, Oklahoma, with their four children.

Q: What is unique about the way pastors use social media in today's culture? How can these platforms be a valuable extension of their role as teachers and leaders?

A: People are sharing more of their lives online, often with more transparency than ever before. As the Church, we have an unprecedented opportunity to love, encourage and bring hope to people beyond the hours when they are physically in church. Whether we're helping someone find the next step in their spiritual growth or reminding someone of who they are in Christ, social media opens up new doors for ministry.

Q: Pastors are nearly split on whether social media has (46%) or has not (54%) affected the way they distribute their time and effort in ministry. What is your advice to pastors who struggle to focus, or who have not figured out how to efficiently incorporate social media into their routines?

A: When new technology is introduced and gains rapid adoption, some degree of cultural disruption inevitably follows. People make wild predictions about its impact on our lives and society, going to utopian or apocalyptic extremes.

You don't have to look too far back into history to see this play out. When the telephone was introduced over 100 years ago, some people responded with excitement and others with fear. Bold declarations were made that the telephone would decimate relationships. Now, because of the amount of time that has passed, we're able to have more perspective on its real impact. Some things did change, but overall, society was able to integrate the technology of the telephone in a way that generally avoided the most extreme predictions.

With a tool as young as social media, we are now navigating the tension between different extremes, such as:

- **Global vs. local:** Who is my neighbor? We can experience real-time communication with people on the other side of the world. What used to be determined by my geographic limitations now has no limits. Is our main responsibility to invest our time in those who are physically near? Or should we seek out the opportunity to reach someone who has never heard the gospel and is outside the reach of any church?

- **Broadcast vs. personal:** With social media, we can connect with more people or connect with people more. In the few moments it takes to compose and publish a post, pastors can communicate to a larger group than might come through the doors of their church each weekend. Or they can keep their focus on individual communication and use social media to enrich relationships by connecting one-on-one more easily and more often.

- **Omnipresent vs. never present:** Social media allows us to be involved in many different ongoing conversations. But if we're always buried in our devices, we might find we're never fully present with the people in front of us. Is it a distraction or an empowerment to be engaged in several places at once?

The introduction of new technology forces us to wrestle with these tensions. Each choice we make comes with a benefit and a cost. As long as we're self-aware and intentional, we can assess the positives and negatives and assimilate these tools in a way that's going to be productive. Instead of living on the edge of the extremes, we can lead the way in defining new norms and boundaries.

Q: What are some general dos and don'ts you recommend to pastors as they explore new methods and technologies in their communication?

A: With any form of technology or innovation, it's easy to focus too much on what we're doing and overlook *why* we're doing it. New methods don't steer our ministry, and we don't jump into them for novelty's sake. We make sure every team member understands that technology is not the center of our ministry. We pursue innovation with purpose, and for us, that purpose is to lead people to become fully devoted followers of Christ. We're going to do everything short of sin to accomplish that.

15. WOMEN

In what ways is pastoring different for women?

In 2016 Hillary Clinton was the first woman to receive a major party's nomination for president of the United States, emblematic of immense social changes for women during the past 50 years. According to Barna's tracking data, a related trend is the slow but steady rise of women clergy in the Protestant community.

One out every 11 Protestant senior pastors is a woman (9%)—triple the percentage of 25 years ago. Most, but by no means all, lead mainline congregations; 44 percent of non-mainline pastors say their denomination, church network or congregation ordains women for pastoral leadership, compared to virtually all mainline pastors (99%).

That does not mean, however, that women with leadership gifts and a ministry calling have no place to serve in non-mainline churches. Barna offered pastors a list of ministry roles that someone might have in a church and asked whether, in their congregation, a woman is permitted to hold that position. Most church leadership positions are, in fact, available to female leaders—but a majority of non-mainline churches opens their most senior positions only to men. About one-third of non-mainline pastors say women may serve as senior pastors or executive pastors or as teaching / preaching pastors in their congregation.

Women often pastor smaller churches than their male colleagues; median attendance at churches pastored by women is 75 people at a weekend service compared to 110 at churches led by men. Additionally, women pastors tend to earn less than men. (The attendance gap likely accounts for some measure of the pay gap, since pastors of smaller congregations tend to be paid less than leaders of larger churches.)

WOMEN OFTEN PASTOR SMALLER CHURCHES THAN THEIR MALE COLLEAGUES

MINISTRY ROLES WOMEN ARE PERMITTED TO HOLD

% "yes" among U.S. Protestant pastors

Ministry Role	% Non-Mainline	% Mainline
Children's pastor / ministry leader	88	99
Women's pastor / ministry leader	85	99
Youth leader	84	99
Adult Bible teacher	83	99
Worship leader / music minister	79	99
Small group pastor / ministry leader	74	99
Deacon / deaconess	64	98
Elder / board member	44	99
Associate pastor	44	98
Teaching / preaching pastor	39	97
Senior / executive pastor	35	99

n=600 U.S. Protestant pastors.

A smaller church means a smaller staff, and three-quarters of female senior pastors either work alone (38%) or with just one other paid ministry staff member (36%). By comparison, nearly half of male senior pastors lead a staff of three or more (48%)—and these larger staffs often include women. While it's most common for women to be senior leaders in small churches, larger congregations have, by virtue of their more extensive resources, more paid ministry opportunities for women. Just 17 percent of churches with attendance of more than 250 have an all-male ministry staff, compared to 38 percent of churches with less than 250.

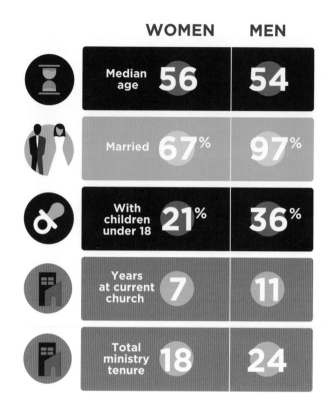

	WOMEN	MEN
Median age	56	54
Married	67%	97%
With children under 18	21%	36%
Years at current church	7	11
Total ministry tenure	18	24

BETTER OFF, WORSE OFF

Beyond matters of demographics and availability of positions, there are some differences in the ways women experience their ministry roles compared to men. Female ministers are less optimistic than their male colleagues when it comes to how they compare with other pastors on matters of work-life balance and their salary-benefits package, but on par with men when it comes to their satisfaction with family support, friendships, job fulfillment and mental / emotional health.

Women are somewhat less likely than men to say they are "better off" compared to other pastors when it comes to their salary and benefits. But much greater is the disparity between women and men on the question of work-life balance. A plurality of men (42%) says they are better off than other U.S. pastors in this regard, but only one-quarter of women pastors believes the same (24%). In this feeling, female pastors are in sync with their peers in the wider workforce; U.S. women overall tend to be less satisfied than men with the balance they manage between career and home life.[22]

Female pastors are more likely than male church leaders to wish they'd been better prepared for people's expectation that they "must do everything" and to say they were not prepared for people to "expect perfection." However, there is no statistical daylight between male and female pastors when it comes to vocational satisfaction; nearly all pastors, regardless of gender, say they are at least somewhat satisfied in their pastoral vocation— and most are very satisfied.

NEARLY ALL PASTORS, REGARDLESS OF GENDER, ARE VERY SATISFIED IN THEIR PASTORAL VOCATION

16. MENTORING

How are pastors engaging with the next generation of church leaders?

Many young Americans expect more than just a paycheck from their career. In particular, Millennials (born between 1984 and 2002) express a desire to make an impact on the world. But with declining church attendance and broader secularizing trends in the U.S., young people are looking less often to vocational ministry as a way to fulfill those desires. For *The State of Pastors*, Barna asked current church leaders about their experience with identifying, recruiting and training young Christians to take up vocational church ministry.

The first step toward mentoring future leaders is finding them, and two out of three current pastors believe identifying suitable candidates is becoming more difficult (69%). About one-quarter agrees strongly that "it's becoming harder to find mature young Christians who want to be pastors" (24%), while a larger contingent agrees somewhat (45%). Pastors of large churches seem to have less of a problem identifying potential leaders (38% disagree with the statement) compared with pastors of small congregations (28%), perhaps because the pool of potential leaders is larger.

TWO OUT OF THREE PASTORS BELIEVE IDENTIFYING FUTURE CHURCH LEADERS IS BECOMING MORE DIFFICULT

The rise in popularity of entrepreneurship among younger generations, and its low barrier to entry, may be contributing factors to the shrinking numbers of young ministry candidates. Social enterprises and tech startups promise talented young Americans exciting and fulfilling work, luring them away from more traditional vocational paths. Seven in 10 pastors feel the weight of this new reality: While only 18 percent strongly agree that "a lot of young leaders seem to think other kinds of work are more important than vocational ministry," more than half agree somewhat (52%). Black pastors, in particular, express strong agreement that young leaders tend to esteem other careers over church ministry.

WHAT PASTORS SAY ABOUT THE NEXT GENERATION OF CHURCH LEADERS

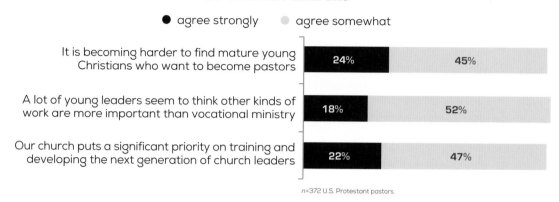

● agree strongly   ● agree somewhat

It is becoming harder to find mature young Christians who want to become pastors — 24% | 45%

A lot of young leaders seem to think other kinds of work are more important than vocational ministry — 18% | 52%

Our church puts a significant priority on training and developing the next generation of church leaders — 22% | 47%

n=372 U.S. Protestant pastors.

That lack of esteem must bother some pastors, especially since most find their ministry vocation so fulfilling. Nine out of 10 say that, based on their own experiences, they would "encourage a young person who is considering a career as a pastor to pursue it" (63% definitely, 29% probably). Those who would probably or definitely not offer such a recommendation tend to be leaders of churches declining in attendance, pastors of color, and less satisfied with their vocation or current church ministry.

Developing suitable young candidates for vocational ministry requires a concerted effort on the part of current pastors and churchgoers, and a majority of pastors believes their church is doing what it takes (69%). Roughly one in five strongly agrees that their church "puts a significant priority on training and developing the next generation of church leaders" (22%), while almost half agree somewhat (47%). This focus appears to be a hallmark of growing congregations: Three-quarters of these pastors agree they prioritize developing young leaders, compared to just over half of those who lead churches with declining attendance.

These development efforts take shape differently in different congregations. When researchers asked pastors to describe one or two specific things their church has done in the past year to identify and develop young leaders, nearly three in 10 said they had hired young staff and / or elected young members to leadership roles (28%), or offered training classes, camps or conferences (27%). One in six reports mentoring a young potential leader (19%), one in nine offered internships or "shadow" roles (11%) and one in 10 led small groups on discipleship and leadership (10%). Slightly rarer actions include giving encouragement and guidance to those who are considering leadership (9%) and putting resources into the youth ministry (7%). According to pastors in the survey:

Children and youth are included in nearly every aspect of our congregation before they even enter school. They serve on ministry teams and council, serve in worship, help plan outreach events, etc. This isn't a token "Aw, look at the kids!" sort of thing; it's part of the congregation's DNA.

We delegate responsibilities to the younger emerging leaders and give them the freedom to fail—with full support.

We are a teaching congregation with a field education student from an area seminary. We also have a scholarship fund for training church leaders, which we have used to fund Bible courses and attendance at leadership training events.

We work with young men and women year-round, putting them in leadership positions. We do not treat them as "the future of the church"—they are an integral part of the church, just like those of us who are older.

Whatever shape it takes, it's imperative for the next generation of pastors to be trained and developed—and most pastors believe the task is getting harder, even as they express deep commitment to getting it done right.

Q&A WITH TERRY LINHART

Q: The teens and early 20s are a pivotal time for most pastors to identify a calling on their lives. What unique events are going on in a person's life during that time that may contribute to such moments of clarity? How can those already in ministry help young people see, learn about and build on their call to ministry?

A: School, parents, peers, grandparents and friends press in during this time and create a swell of pressure on young adults to figure out their vocational identity. The years from 16 to 22 are also the first moments when young people "watch themselves" in an adult world, to see where their interests and gifting intersect with opportunity and a sense of calling. These factors lead to a process of experimentation with various ideas and options, ideally alongside an intense quest to discern what God would have them do.

Those of us who come alongside young adults during these years can help create a "safe place" for them to experiment, discuss and change their minds about the future. There are no external how-to formulas for everyone or "right" answers for every life, yet young adults often feel pressure to have to find *the* answer during this time. The reality is they just have to find the *next* answer that is faithful to God's leading in their lives. So, the best thing we can do is to help them connect more deeply to God, facilitating opportunities for his Spirit to work in their lives.

Q: In your conversations with pastors over the years, what do they describe when they talk about having been "called"? What are some common experiences, feelings or phrases related to this moment of revelation or decision?

A: Calling is not rooted in a desire to be involved in "religious work," but rather in a personal response to a personal God.

TERRY LINHART

Terry Linhart, PhD, is professor of Christian ministries at Bethel College in Mishawaka, Indiana. A speaker and consultant, he is also author of eight books, including *The Self-Aware Leader*. Terry is the founder of Arbor Research Group, a consulting firm that provides unique research and support to Christian organizations, churches and schools.

Young men and women describe that personal call as having an "impression" or a "word" or "they just *knew*." I have the privilege of teaching those who have been called into pastoral ministry. As I listen to their stories, a consistent word is "encounter" with Jesus Christ.

Not all describe it as a single point in time, however. Some prefer the language of process. God prompts their hearts, but then the young person begins a journey of confirmation with others, with circumstances and with opportunities.

Regardless of the circumstances, there is almost always a sacramental quality to the process. Young people often point to a sign God used to confirm or direct their personal calling. It's often something unrelated to more obvious elements of vocational exploration. It could be a "random" conversation, a chance meeting, a symbol, a specific answer to prayer, a sign from nature (for example, the weather) or something they read. And then *they just knew*.

When they receive that final confirmation after considering it for some time, they *know* and make the decision to step forward with confidence.

Q: What is it about time and experience that lends credibility to one's ministry calling?
A: There are three factors that contribute to growing confidence over time: a clear call that can't be easily dismissed, a strong community with others who are in ministry and the loving support of the church community.

The clearer the call is, the greater the confidence. Men and women who can say, "This is what I'm to be about" will never lack confidence. Clarity can come from the external circumstances surrounding one's call (for example, it is tied to an event like summer camp) or from depth of conviction or purpose ("I am called to children's ministry").

Second, too often pastors feel isolated and alone; it's difficult to be "real" with those in our congregations. However, if a pastor gathers regularly with those who share their experience—that is, other pastors—their companionship provides needed perspective on the call to ministry and ministry's reality.

Finally, in my work with African American congregations, I am struck by how intentional many are about honoring their pastor and the pastor's family. There is often a greater formality, along with regular affirmation of the pastor's role and value to the church. It's a stark contrast to what I see in other congregations, where the pastor can end up more of a target than a treasure. The support of their congregation plays an integral role in the growth and confidence of a pastor who endeavors to answer God's call to ministry.

17. PARTNERSHIPS

How important are denominations and other area congregations to a church's ministry?

Many individual churches function in a larger ecosystem of affiliation or relationships, and researchers wanted to assess the strength and extent of this web of connections. Eight out of 10 pastors say their church's relationship with its denomination or church affiliation is either "very" (49%) or "somewhat strong" (31%). Perhaps counterintuitively, non-mainline leaders (53%) are more likely than mainline pastors (37%) to characterize the relationship as very strong. One might assume that a more ecclesiastical, rather than congregational, model of governance would naturally lead to a stronger relationship. But this finding suggests that shared theology may be a more powerful tie than institutional polity when it comes to individual churches and their parent denomination.

Small churches and midsize congregations also report stronger associations with their denomination compared to large churches. Additionally, pastors who earn less than $40,000 per year are more apt than those who earn $60,000 or more to describe their denominational relationship as very strong.

Interestingly, pastors who are very satisfied with their vocation or with their current church ministry tend to report a very strong relationship with their denomination compared to those who are less satisfied. The cause of these correlations is unclear, but it's possible that satisfied, less-stressed leaders feel supported by the denominational apparatus, rather than micromanaged or stifled.

A strong relationship does not necessarily mean the denomination exerts great influence on a church's day-to-day activities. In fact, non-mainline pastors (who are most likely to report very

SHARED THEOLOGY MAY BE A MORE POWERFUL TIE THAN INSTITUTIONAL POLITY WHEN IT COMES TO CHURCHES AND THEIR DENOMINATION

strong ties) are three times more likely than mainline leaders to describe the denomination's daily influence as "none at all" (22% vs. 7% mainline).

Overall, just one-quarter of all pastors says their denomination has "a lot" of influence (23%) and one-third says "some" (34%). Pastors of color (48%) are far more likely than white ministers (20%) to say their denomination has a lot of sway over their day-to-day ministry activities and decisions—yet they are no more likely than whites to describe their denominational ties as very strong.

HOW OFTEN CHURCH PARTNERS WITH OTHER AREA CHURCHES, BY PASTOR'S ETHNICITY

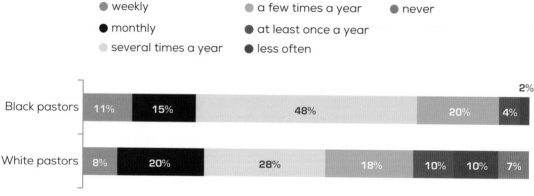

- weekly
- monthly
- several times a year
- a few times a year
- at least once a year
- less often
- never

Black pastors: 11% | 15% | 48% | 20% | 4% | 2%

White pastors: 8% | 20% | 28% | 18% | 10% | 10% | 7%

n=525 U.S. Protestant pastors.

LOCAL PARTNERSHIPS

Ethnicity also seems to be a factor in a pastor's inclination to partner with other area churches, even though they may belong to a different denomination. Black church leaders, in particular, report doing so more often than white pastors: Nearly half say they do so "several times a year" (48%), 20 points more than white leaders who say the same. And they are less likely to say they "never" partner with other local churches or that they do so less often than once a year.

There is some evidence that low engagement with other congregations in the local community correlates both to smaller church size and to declining attendance. One in five pastors of small churches (21%) and one in four pastors of churches with declining attendance (25%) say they never or only rarely partner with other congregations. By comparison, only about 10 percent of midsize church pastors and 15 percent of those who lead growing churches report similar levels of low engagement.

All in all, it appears that a relatively strong web of connections, both to the denominational network and to other local communities of faith, often correlates to church health and pastoral health—suggesting that pastors and network leaders should evaluate what's working best on these fronts and consider how to fortify and extend these partnerships.

A RELATIVELY STRONG WEB OF CONNECTIONS OFTEN CORRELATES TO CHURCH HEALTH AND PASTOR HEALTH

18. SATISFACTION

What part of their job do pastors enjoy most?

Throughout *The State of Pastors* we refer to church leaders who are "very satisfied" (or not) with their vocation and who are "very satisfied" (or not) specifically with their ministry in their current church. But how many pastors fall into these categories?

Most pastors are, in fact, content. Seven in 10 U.S. Protestant pastors say they are very satisfied with their pastoral vocation (72%). One-quarter says they are "somewhat satisfied" (25%), and the remaining 3 percent admit they are "not too" or "not at all" satisfied.

When it comes to satisfaction with their current church ministry, the numbers paint a less rosy picture: Roughly half of all pastors are very satisfied (53%), two in five are somewhat satisfied (41%) and 7 percent are not too or not at all satisfied.

Barna analysts grouped together the pastors who are less than very satisfied into discrete population segments to see if these leaders have factors in common that are different from those who express the highest level of satisfaction. And, as we have already seen in this report, vocational satisfaction and satisfaction in one's current church make an impact on many other measures of a pastor's well-being. The inverse is also true: Low measures of well-being in various areas of life and ministry have an effect on a pastor's levels of satisfaction.

Leaders who are 50 and older are more apt than younger pastors to say they are very satisfied, both with vocation and with their current church. Relatedly, pastors who have been in ministry for 30 years or longer tend to say they are very satisfied vocationally and in their current position, especially compared to leaders who have been in ministry between 15 and 29 years.

VOCATIONAL SATISFACTION MAKES AN IMPACT ON MANY OTHER MEASURES OF A PASTOR'S WELL-BEING

In "Risk" (see pp. 20), analysis suggests that some measure of pastors' mental and emotional health is predicated on the growth or decline of their church's attendance. Strengthening that contention is the relationship between a pastor's satisfaction and the direction of their church's attendance numbers: As a rule, those who lead growing churches are more satisfied and those who lead declining churches are less so.

SATISFACTION WITH VOCATION, BY CHURCH ATTENDANCE

● very satisfied　　● somewhat satisfied　　● not too / not at all satisfied

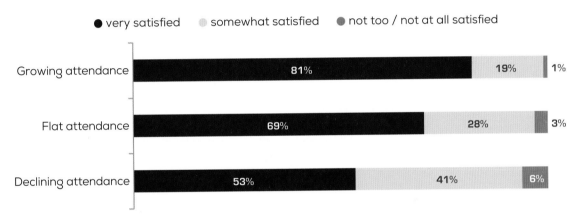

Growing attendance: 81% | 19% | 1%
Flat attendance: 69% | 28% | 3%
Declining attendance: 53% | 41% | 6%

SATISFACTION WITH CURRENT CHURCH, BY CHURCH ATTENDANCE

● very satisfied　　● somewhat satisfied　　● not too / not at all satisfied

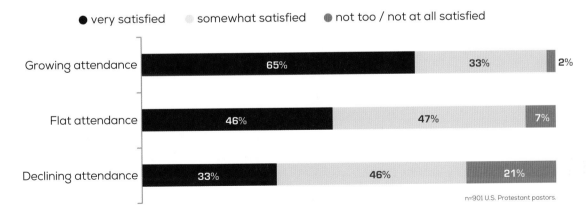

Growing attendance: 65% | 33% | 2%
Flat attendance: 46% | 47% | 7%
Declining attendance: 33% | 46% | 21%

n=901 U.S. Protestant pastors.

WHAT PASTORS LIKE BEST

When asked to choose just one pastoral task as their favorite from a list of ministry activities, two-thirds of senior church leaders say they most enjoy "preaching and teaching" (66%). Given that the sermon or message is the centerpiece of most Protestant worship services, this comes as no surprise.

There is a big drop-off from there. One in 10 says "developing other leaders" is their most enjoyable task (10%), and one in 12 prefers "discipling believers" (8%). "Evangelizing" (6%) and "pastoral care" (5%) bring the most joy to smaller proportions of pastors, and a mere 2 percent say they enjoy "organizing church events, meetings or ministries."

Unexpectedly, church size seems to have an influence on what task a pastor most enjoys. Leaders of small churches of less than 100 weekend attenders are more likely than large-church pastors to choose discipling believers and evangelizing or sharing the gospel. Those who lead large churches with 250 or more members, by contrast, enjoy preaching and teaching even more than the average.

As we saw in "Communication" (pp. 76), leaders of small churches tend to be more personally accessible to their congregants than large-church pastors—and the findings here may indicate they prefer it that way. Discipleship, sharing the gospel and pastoral care are oftentimes best done one on one or in small, tight-knit groups. And many who lead small churches appear well-suited for these relational ministry activities.

MINISTRY ACTIVITIES PASTORS MOST ENJOY, BY CHURCH SIZE

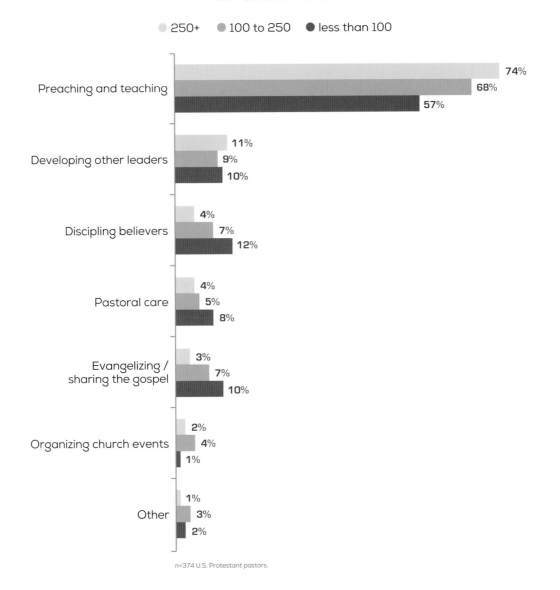

● 250+   ● 100 to 250   ● less than 100

Preaching and teaching
- 74%
- 68%
- 57%

Developing other leaders
- 11%
- 9%
- 10%

Discipling believers
- 4%
- 7%
- 12%

Pastoral care
- 4%
- 5%
- 8%

Evangelizing / sharing the gospel
- 3%
- 7%
- 10%

Organizing church events
- 2%
- 4%
- 1%

Other
- 1%
- 3%
- 2%

n=374 U.S. Protestant pastors.

THE UPS AND DOWNS

Most, but not all, U.S. senior pastors are very satisfied with their calling, ministry and current church. Pastoring is not all roses and sunshine, however, even for those who are most content. Here's a look at the best parts of the job—and the not-so-great parts.

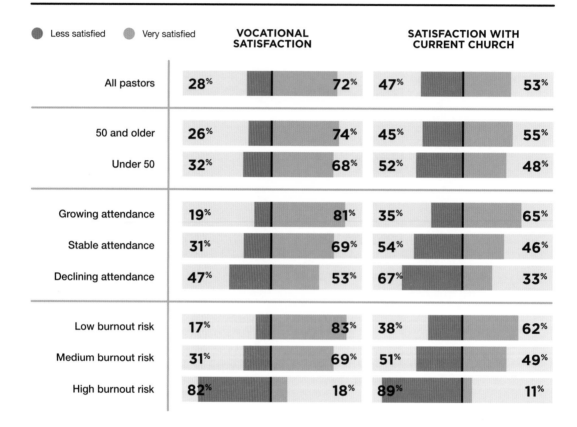

Legend: ● Less satisfied ● Very satisfied

VOCATIONAL SATISFACTION | **SATISFACTION WITH CURRENT CHURCH**

	Less / Very satisfied (Vocational)	Less / Very satisfied (Current Church)
All pastors	28% / 72%	47% / 53%
50 and older	26% / 74%	45% / 55%
Under 50	32% / 68%	52% / 48%
Growing attendance	19% / 81%	35% / 65%
Stable attendance	31% / 69%	54% / 46%
Declining attendance	47% / 53%	67% / 33%
Low burnout risk	17% / 83%	38% / 62%
Medium burnout risk	31% / 69%	51% / 49%
High burnout risk	82% / 18%	89% / 11%

PASTORS LOVE . . .

Senior church leaders enjoy many different aspects of being a pastor. But if they have to pick just one, a majority says nothing holds a candle to delivering the weekly message.

66%	10%	8%	6%	5%	2%	2%
Preaching and teaching	Developing other leaders	Discipling believers	Evangelizing / sharing the gospel	Pastoral care	Organizing church events	Other

19. FRUSTRATION
THE WORST PART OF MY JOB

Frustrations with apathetic parishioners top the list.

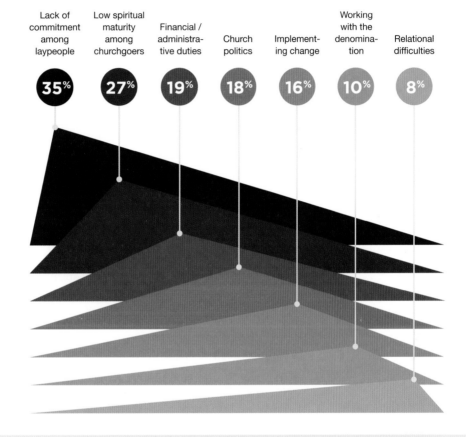

Lack of commitment among laypeople	Low spiritual maturity among churchgoers	Financial / administrative duties	Church politics	Implementing change	Working with the denomination	Relational difficulties
35%	27%	19%	18%	16%	10%	8%

PASTORS ARE GOOD AT . . .

Most pastors love to preach—and a majority thinks they're pretty good at it, too. Here's how many rate themselves as "excellent" on each pastoral task.

57%	29%	29%	24%	14%	10%	6%
Preaching and teaching	Connecting with neighbor-hood / city	Leading the organization	Counseling / pastoral care	Mentoring younger leaders	Evangelizing / sharing the gospel	Mobilizing volunteers

n=374 U.S. Protestant pastors.

What frustrates pastors most about ministry?

Even the most energizing, rewarding job has its downsides—and while pastors generally report higher levels of satisfaction than U.S. adults overall, the job of pastoring is no exception. Given an opportunity to identify the one or two biggest downsides of their job, the top five frustrations reported by pastors are:

1. Lack of commitment among laypeople (35%)
2. Low level of spiritual maturity among churchgoers (27%)
3. Financial and / or administrative duties (19%)
4. Church politics (18%)
5. Implementing change in the church (16%)

Lack of laity commitment also topped the list of frustrations in George Barna's 1992 study of senior pastors, followed by financial and administrative duties and "how to do effective outreach." [23]

In 2017, lack of commitment and spiritual maturity are the top choices of nearly all segments, including pastors high on the burnout risk and relational risk metrics. However, for at-risk leaders, church politics and financial / administrative duties are particularly frustrating, especially when compared with those who rank low on the risk metrics. For example, pastors at high risk of burnout are three times more likely than those at low risk to say church politics is among their top frustrations.

When it comes to job headaches, there are a handful of significant differences between leaders in churches of various sizes. Pastors of small congregations, for example, are burdened by administrative duties more frequently than leaders of midsize or large churches. At the other end of the spectrum, pastors of large churches are more apt than the norm to be irritated by "working with the denomination"—perhaps because their churches are too big to fly under the organizational radar.

The frustrations common among midsize church leaders seem to indicate a challenging "in-between" phase of leadership.

PASTORS' TOP FRUSTRATIONS, 2017 VS. 1992

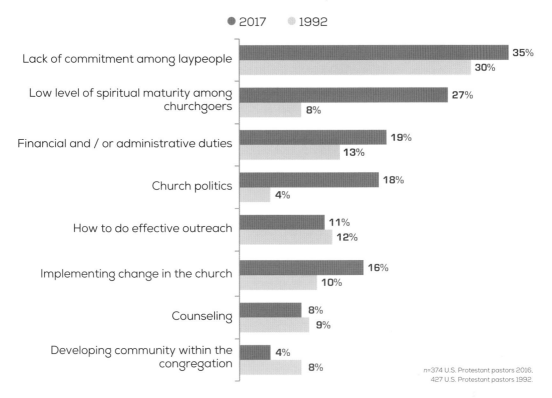

● 2017   ● 1992

Lack of commitment among laypeople — 35% / 30%

Low level of spiritual maturity among churchgoers — 27% / 8%

Financial and / or administrative duties — 19% / 13%

Church politics — 18% / 4%

How to do effective outreach — 11% / 12%

Implementing change in the church — 16% / 10%

Counseling — 8% / 9%

Developing community within the congregation — 4% / 8%

*n=374 U.S. Protestant pastors 2016,
427 U.S. Protestant pastors 1992.*

Implementing change in the church and church politics are bigger headaches for these leaders than for pastors of large congregations. They are also more prone to frustration over the low level of spiritual maturity in their congregation compared to both small- and large-church pastors.

Every pastor, regardless of church size or job satisfaction, has frustrations related to the daily reality of congregational life. And that's okay. The trick is to acknowledge irritations without letting them fill one's field of vision. When frustrations get too big or too close, they distort perception and make daily joys appear small and inconsequential—which is an apt description of burnout. How can pastors deal well with pastoral disappointments so they don't lead to vocational weariness?

EVERY PASTOR, REGARDLESS OF CHURCH SIZE OR JOB SATISFACTION, HAS FRUSTRATIONS RELATED TO THE DAILY REALITY OF CONGREGATIONAL LIFE

20. FIT

How well do pastors' day-to-day tasks fit with their calling and gifts?

Unless they are one of the few who preside over a large church with a pastoral staff that can specialize in various aspects of ministry and church administration, senior pastors are jacks-of-all-trades who wear a number of hats: preacher, teacher, theologian, evangelist, counselor, executive and PR spokesperson, to name just a few functions. But pastors are not superhuman, and each is better at some parts of the job than others.

Researchers asked pastors to rate how well they perform certain aspects of their demanding roles, and to assess how well their primary tasks fit into their sense of calling and giftedness. Most say they are well-suited to their role, and they overwhelmingly believe their greatest competence is as thought leaders, indicating strengths in preaching, Bible knowledge and theology.

Nearly all pastors believe their primary tasks—*where they spend the greatest amount of their time and energy*—fit their sense of calling and giftedness either "very well" (55%) or "somewhat well" (42%). Just 4 percent say their primary tasks do not fit them very well.

Those who have been in ministry for 30 years or longer are more confident of their fit than those who are newer to ministry. Similar patterns are found among pastors at various points on the burnout and spiritual risk metrics.

When it comes to specific tasks and skillsets, pastors overwhelmingly rate themselves better on "preaching and teaching" than any other part of the job. Nearly six in 10 rate themselves as excellent (57%) and about one-third as good (36%) on this aspect of their role. A close second is "knowledge of scripture" (48%

> **MOST PASTORS BELIEVE THEIR GREATEST COMPETENCE IS AS THOUGHT LEADERS, INDICATING STRENGTHS IN PREACHING, BIBLE KNOWLEDGE AND THEOLOGY**

PASTORS' FIT ASSESSMENT, BY RISK METRICS

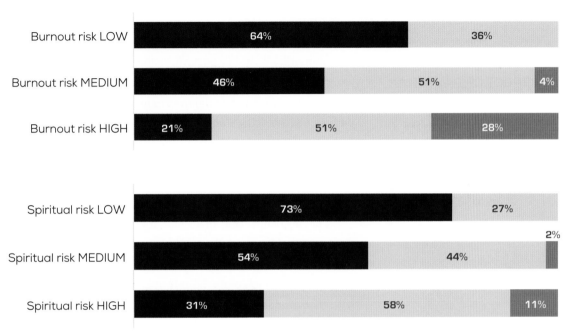

● fit very well   ○ fit somewhat well   ● fit not very / not at all well

Burnout risk LOW	64%	36%	
Burnout risk MEDIUM	46%	51%	4%
Burnout risk HIGH	21%	51%	28%
Spiritual risk LOW	73%	27%	
Spiritual risk MEDIUM	54%	44%	2%
Spiritual risk HIGH	31%	58%	11%

n=900 U.S. Protestant pastors.

excellent, 45% good), followed closely by "practical or applied the-ology" (42% excellent, 48% good). These skills fall under the broad umbrella of *thought leadership*, which dominates the self-reported ratings.

The next category of pastoral skills is *organizational leader-ship,* which includes "leading the organization," "managing the church's finances" and "managing the staff." Three in 10 pastors rate themselves as excellent at leading the organization, with those who lead growing churches more likely to say so than those whose growth trajectory is declining or flat. Roughly the same propor-tion, three in 10, say they are excellent at managing their church's finances (28%); pastors who manage an annual church budget of $1 million or more are especially inclined to rate themselves high on this aspect of the job (51%). Fewer pastors rate themselves as excellent when it comes to managing the staff (16%), and those who do tend to lead churches with 250 or more people in attendance (22%), which are more likely than small congregations to employ a large ministry staff.

When it comes to connecting with the church's surrounding community, pastors who have led their church for 10 or more years are more apt, as one might expect, than those who are new to their community to rate themselves as excellent. As a corollary finding, pastors with a shorter church tenure rate themselves lower overall on "evangelizing people" than those who have pastored their current church for at least 10 years, perhaps because they are still in the process of forming relationships in their neighborhood.

The data show that most pastors believe they fit well in their role. It's also clear they tend to see themselves primarily as thought leaders. There is certainly an upside to this focus, since the weekly sermon is often the only interaction congregants have with their senior pastor; it's fitting, then, that pastors feel most confident in the task that touches, and hopefully persuades or encourages, the greatest number of people.

Yet, in another sense, the laser-like focus on preaching and teaching could be problematic, if there are not additional staff and volunteers to meet the church's broader pastoral needs. A senior pastor does not have to be an excellent counselor in order to be a good pastor, but someone with this gift needs to come alongside him or her to offer congregants wise counsel and relational guidance. Thus, one important aspect of pastoral leadership is recognizing one's weaknesses and empowering others to take up the ministry slack.

Are pastors up to the task? Part III widens the scope of assessment to include the general population's perceptions of pastors and their ministries, and explores the complex, accelerated environment in which pastors must now lead.

ONE IMPORTANT ASPECT OF PASTORAL LEADERSHIP IS RECOGNIZING ONE'S WEAKNESSES AND EMPOWERING OTHERS TO TAKE UP THE MINISTRY SLACK

HOW PASTORS RATE THEMSELVES ON MINISTRY TASKS

% "excellent" among U.S. Protestant pastors

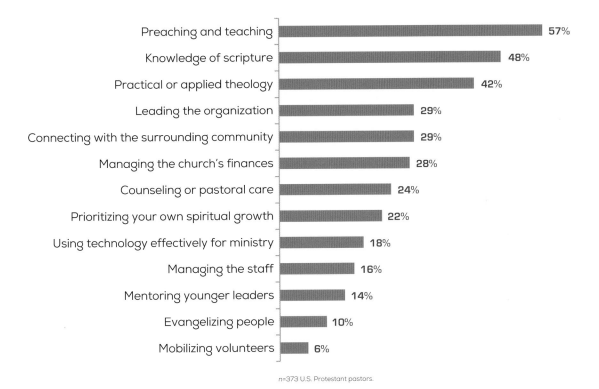

Task	%
Preaching and teaching	57%
Knowledge of scripture	48%
Practical or applied theology	42%
Leading the organization	29%
Connecting with the surrounding community	29%
Managing the church's finances	28%
Counseling or pastoral care	24%
Prioritizing your own spiritual growth	22%
Using technology effectively for ministry	18%
Managing the staff	16%
Mentoring younger leaders	14%
Evangelizing people	10%
Mobilizing volunteers	6%

n=373 U.S. Protestant pastors.

PART III

CULTURAL LEADERSHIP

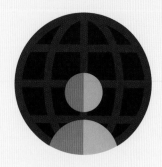

CULTURAL LEADERSHIP

Part I looked at how pastors relate to themselves, to God and to the people closest to them. Part II examined the dynamics of leadership in congregational life. Part III now turns to the wider context in which pastors lead: the complex, accelerated culture where churches are called to be God's people. Historically, pastors have been among the most influential leaders in the nation's life. Is that still true today? What is changing about a pastor's role in cultural leadership?

How effective are churches at evangelism and discipleship? How are pastors perceived by the average American? Do people think church leaders are good for their community and reliable guides for life? What are the qualities of a good pastor? How does a non-ministry career compare with a pastoral calling? How do pastors view their church's role in racial justice? Are they concerned about religious freedom? What would people like to learn from pastors? What is the toughest part of pastoring in today's culture?

Throughout Part III we explore various facets of cultural complexity that make leading a church challenging in new ways, and examine how pastors can develop resilience in the face of so much change.

U.S. adults are ambivalent about "pastors" but like their pastor.

Just one-quarter has a very positive opinion of Christian ministers as a group, but two-thirds who personally know a pastor give him or her high marks.

1 IN 5 | People don't think pastors have much influence.
One in five U.S. adults says the pastors in their community are very influential.

Pastors perceive the culture's growing indifference.

Only 22% would say the respect clergymembers are afforded by their community is excellent; 7 in 10 say it's merely good or average.

Most people believe pastors are beneficial for their community.

Church leaders may not wield enormous influence, but most folks consider them a benefit for their town or city.

21% | U.S. adults aren't sure pastors are a credible source of wisdom.
Only one in five says they are very credible on today's issues—and fewer when it comes to issues of faith and politics.

Pastors and U.S. adults agree on the top traits of good pastor.

Both groups say love for God and love for people are the most important pastoral attributes.

Nearly all pastors say churches play an important role in racial reconciliation.

But only half say it is among their church's priorities.

85% | A majority of pastors believes religious freedom is weakening.
And most believe it's likely that Christians' ability to practice their faith will be restricted in the next decade.

People believe churches can meet their community's needs.

Especially when it comes to material and spiritual needs, U.S. adults are hopeful about how churches can help.

Most pastors don't feel prepared to teach cultural engagement.

Only 1 in 3 says they are very prepared to teach their members how to engage in constructive conversations with people who disagree with them on sensitive social issues.

At a Glance

21. OUTREACH
OUTCOMES OF OUTREACH

How often, and how well, are churches engaging in service and evangelism to their communities?

5

The average number of service projects a church conducts each year

Understandably, a church's size and financial resources impact its ability to conduct outreach.

Annual Budget	Service Projects / Year
< $100K ▶	3
$100K to $249K ▶	4
$250K to $999K ▶	5
$1M+ ▶	10

Attendance	Service Projects / Year
< 100 adults ▶	4
100 to 249 adults ▶	5
250+ adults ▶	8

IS IT WORKING?

● Very effective ● Somewhat effective ● Not very effective ● Not at all effective

A majority of pastors report their church is just "somewhat" effective (or less) at reaching out to unchurched people.

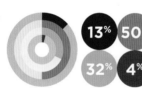

13% 50%
32% 4%

Even so, pastors feel mostly optimistic about their church's efforts in discipleship and spiritual formation.

14% 73%
12% 1%

Whether or not their outreach approach seems productive, most pastors say the size of their congregation has either grown or remained stable in the past year.

● Increased
● Decreased
● Stayed the same

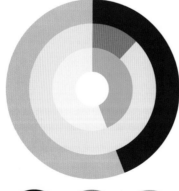

44% 12% 44%

12

AVERAGE NEW BELIEVERS ANNUALLY

10

AVERAGE BAPTISMS ANNUALLY

How effective are churches at evangelism and discipleship?

For many churches, particularly those who consider themselves evangelical, outreach is central to the idea of "cultural leadership." After all, making disciples was the risen Christ's Great Commission to his followers—a commission that, if wholly fulfilled, would undeniably transform culture. So how do pastors think their churches are doing when it comes to outreach and growing disciples?

Most are apt to think their church is more effective at discipleship than at evangelism and outreach. Nearly nine out of 10 rate their church's discipleship or spiritual formation efforts as "very" (14%) or "somewhat effective" (73%), compared to two-thirds who say so about their church "reaching out to unchurched people" (13% very, 50% somewhat effective).

Note that, on both counts, the percentage that rates their congregation as *very* effective is comparatively small. However, black pastors tend to rate their congregations better than the national norm on outreach (25%). And one in five pastors of growing churches say their congregation is very effective at both outreach (21%) and discipleship (22%), compared to just 4 percent of pastors who helm churches with declining attendance.

When it comes to the effectiveness of their discipleship ministry, leaders of large churches are in the same statistical ballpark as those who lead small and midsize congregations, but are far more likely to say they are very effective at outreach to the unchurched (20% large vs. 14% small, 9% midsize).

There is also a fairly stark split between mainline and non-mainline churches when it comes to outreach effectiveness. Less than half of mainline pastors say their church is effective at reaching out to unchurched people (9% very, 37% somewhat), compared to seven in 10 non-mainline leaders (15% very, 55% somewhat).

MOST PASTORS ARE APT TO THINK THEIR CHURCH IS MORE EFFECTIVE AT DISCIPLESHIP THAN AT EVANGELISM AND OUTREACH

NUMBER & PURPOSE OF SERVICE PROJECTS

Most congregations do a handful of service projects each year that are designed to serve people outside of their church body; the average (median) number of projects completed in the last 12 months is five. There is, of course, a wide range of variation: 3 percent of pastors say their church did more than 50 service initiatives in the past year, while 5 percent report no such events.

Not surprisingly, church size and budget are factors here. One in nine churches with fewer than 100 adult attenders, and 17 percent of churches with an annual budget of less than $100,000, did not complete any service projects in the last 12 months. On the other hand, large churches and congregations with a budget of $1 million or more completed an average of eight and 10 events last year, respectively, and none of them report having done none at all.

Regardless of church size, there is broad consensus that the main goals of community service are "loving / serving others as Jesus taught," "being the hands and feet of Jesus" and "outreach / evangelism to the people we serve." The last of these is more of a priority among non-mainline pastors than mainline, but "embodying the kingdom of God" is a greater concern for mainline pastors than non-mainline.

There are also a few notable differences between younger and older pastors. Leaders under 50 are more prone to prioritize outreach and evangelism and blessing their neighborhood, while leaders 50 and older are especially keen to help their congregation act as "the hands and feet of Jesus."

MOST CONGREGATIONS DO
A HANDFUL OF SERVICE
PROJECTS EACH YEAR TO
SERVE PEOPLE OUTSIDE
OF THEIR CHURCH BODY

MAIN GOALS OF COMMUNITY SERVICE, BY DENOMINATION AND PASTOR'S AGE

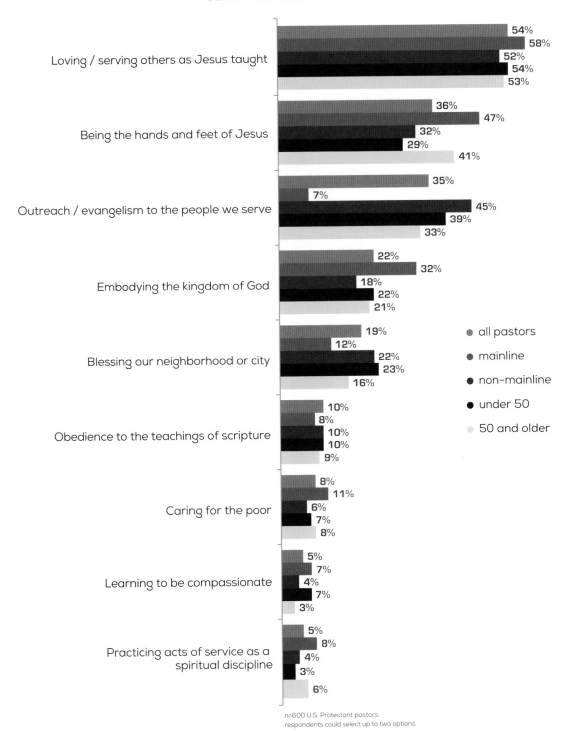

Loving / serving others as Jesus taught
- 54%
- 58%
- 52%
- 54%
- 53%

Being the hands and feet of Jesus
- 36%
- 47%
- 32%
- 29%
- 41%

Outreach / evangelism to the people we serve
- 35%
- 7%
- 45%
- 39%
- 33%

Embodying the kingdom of God
- 22%
- 32%
- 18%
- 22%
- 21%

Blessing our neighborhood or city
- 19%
- 12%
- 22%
- 23%
- 16%

Obedience to the teachings of scripture
- 10%
- 8%
- 10%
- 10%
- 9%

Caring for the poor
- 8%
- 11%
- 6%
- 7%
- 8%

Learning to be compassionate
- 5%
- 7%
- 4%
- 7%
- 3%

Practicing acts of service as a spiritual discipline
- 5%
- 8%
- 4%
- 3%
- 6%

Legend:
- all pastors
- mainline
- non-mainline
- under 50
- 50 and older

n=600 U.S. Protestant pastors; respondents could select up to two options.

Q&A WITH SHARON HOOVER

SHARON HOOVER

Sharon R. Hoover is director of missions at Centreville Presbyterian Church in Centreville, Virginia, where she develops partnerships and equips the congregation to connect with mission partners. In her 20 years on church staffs, she has traveled extensively to lead teams alongside domestic and global partners. Sharon writes and speaks on missions, discipleship and living a faith-filled life in the world God loves. Her current project is a book to guide people in their search for effective missional engagement. Sharon lives in the Washington, DC, area with her husband and occasionally visiting college children.

Q: How would you advise pastors to identify international and local needs that their congregation is uniquely equipped or called to partner with?

A: To identify your congregation's callings, first consider the missions and outreaches you did over the past year. What drew the most support from members / attendees? What received little contribution? For example: Did the collection for school supplies for impoverished children draw an abundance of donations? Did the request for canned goods fill the church lobby with hundreds of pounds of food? Did the special collection for your missionary planting churches in Nepal receive funds far beyond expectations?

Second, listen to congregation members as they talk about their activities outside the church. Do they love volunteering in schools? Do they garden? Are they woodworkers? Do they have a heart for the elderly? What about employment—does your congregation have an abundance of lawyers, engineers, police officers or teachers? Consider distributing a short survey to ask about hobbies, interests and employment.

Then, put it all together. While asking these questions of my current congregation, a heart for "vulnerable children" rose to the surface. Several families foster children, others are adoptive parents. Many members sponsor children with mission organizations. Special collections for children's needs drew tremendous responses. We began investing more with our local and international partners who focus on meeting the needs of vulnerable children. Now more congregation members join in and even create new opportunities to serve, from mentoring children in the local school to serving on mission teams with international partners.

Q: What do you see as metrics for success when pastors are evaluating their church's service and outreach ministries?

A: Metrics are an accountability tool. By themselves, they are a neutral collection of numbers. When accumulated over time, however, metrics provide valuable insights of change. Trends emerge to reveal outcomes far beyond the initial lists of funds raised, in-kind donations given, number of volunteer hours served, and so on. In no particular order, helpful measures include the number of:

- Professions of faith and baptisms
- Participants (in an event or with a mission opportunity)
- Members / attendees trained to share their faith stories and the gospel message
- Annual mission opportunities
- Mission partners who share via video, Skype, in person or written articles to update the congregation on their ministry
- Members / attendees who go to the next level of involvement with mission partners

Just as significant, yet difficult to quantify, are the incremental moments of progress in missional engagement. How do we quantify starting a spiritual conversation with a neighbor, inviting a friend to your small group or exploring first steps with a mission partner? These moments are best celebrated through story. The metric then is to ask, *Do we have a story this week of God's hand at work and our willing response?*

Q: A church's smaller size and budget can be barriers to service and mission projects. What are some simple or low-cost ways to engage in outreach?
A: People want to give time to outreaches that make an impact. Connect with your mission partners to learn their needs, both locally and globally, then explore ways to meet their needs through the abilities and passions of your congregation. Be open to new expressions of outreach as well as reruns of older yet still-needed projects. When we create opportunities that matter, people are willing to join in the work.

Congregation members / attendees have a wide range of financial and time availability. Whether a single mom or an empty nester, people want to serve. To best engage them, offer a variety of outreach options. Not only will a range of opportunities provide ways to explore the members' best fit and calling, they will allow a natural progression for your church family to deepen their connection with your mission partners. For example: In your partnership with a local homeless shelter, a member could donate a dozen oranges, bake a hot casserole, join the rotation to serve breakfast monthly, contribute to their building fund, join their social media team to raise awareness about local poverty or lead the shelter's weekly Bible study. From an addition on the grocery list to weekly engagement, these types of opportunities offer numerous ways to engage with your mission partners.

22. IMPRESSIONS
POP-CULTURE PASTORS

Christian ministers have been portrayed in the media as heroes, villains and everything in between. How similar are those portrayals to Americans' personal experience with pastors?

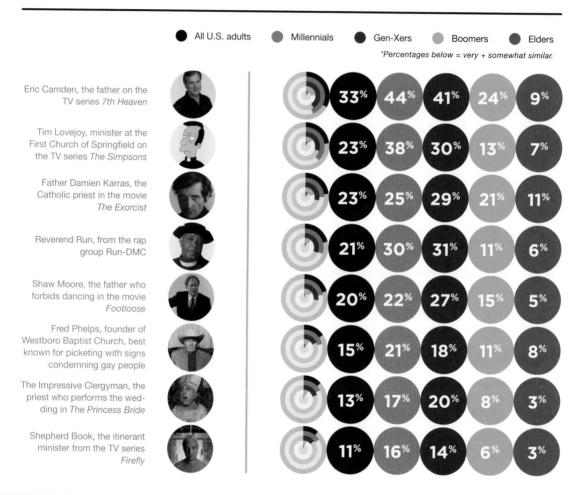

● All U.S. adults ● Millennials ● Gen-Xers ● Boomers ● Elders

Percentages below = very + somewhat similar.

Eric Camden, the father on the TV series *7th Heaven*
33% | 44% | 41% | 24% | 9%

Tim Lovejoy, minister at the First Church of Springfield on the TV series *The Simpsons*
23% | 38% | 30% | 13% | 7%

Father Damien Karras, the Catholic priest in the movie *The Exorcist*
23% | 25% | 29% | 21% | 11%

Reverend Run, from the rap group Run-DMC
21% | 30% | 31% | 11% | 6%

Shaw Moore, the father who forbids dancing in the movie *Footloose*
20% | 22% | 27% | 15% | 5%

Fred Phelps, founder of Westboro Baptist Church, best known for picketing with signs condemning gay people
15% | 21% | 18% | 11% | 8%

The Impressive Clergyman, the priest who performs the wedding in *The Princess Bride*
13% | 17% | 20% | 8% | 3%

Shepherd Book, the itinerant minister from the TV series *Firefly*
11% | 16% | 14% | 6% | 3%

Has your personal, real-life experience of Christian ministers been more favorable, less favorable or about the same as how the media portrays pastors, priests and other ministers?

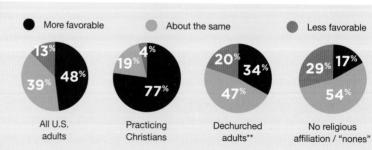

● More favorable ● About the same ● Less favorable

All U.S. adults
13% | 39% | 48%

Practicing Christians
4% | 19% | 77%

Dechurched adults**
20% | 47% | 34%

No religious affiliation / "nones"
17% | 29% | 54%

n=1,025 U.S. adults 18 and older. **Dechurched adults attended church in the past, but not within the last six months.

How are pastors perceived by the average American?

When researchers decided to put together a "pastors in pop culture" series of questions for U.S. adults, the task's unexpected difficulty was a reminder of our culture's ever-increasing complexity. *Fragmentation* is just one aspect of this complexity. There are no longer TV shows that "everybody" watches or movies that "everyone" has seen. Because media content today is niche-driven, micro-targeted and on-demand, Barna had to reach "into the vault," so to speak, to find pop-culture pastors with whom a majority of Americans might be familiar.

Whether someone has a passing familiarity with *The Simpsons'* Reverend Tim Lovejoy is not particularly significant. What *is* significant is the extent to which pastors (real ones) have dropped off the radar as a cultural force. The problem is not that the average American has an overwhelmingly negative perception of Christian ministers; it's that the average American doesn't think about them at all.

Just one-quarter of all U.S. adults says their overall opinion of pastors in general is "very positive" (24%). On the other hand, roughly the same proportion holds a negative opinion (9% very, 19% somewhat). But the largest single share is the 48 percent of Americans whose opinion is "somewhat positive." Most don't actively hate pastors, not at all. They just don't especially care.

The news is somewhat better when it comes to pastors whom people know personally, rather than "pastors" as a general idea. More than half of U.S. adults say they personally are "very" (32%) or "somewhat familiar" (26%) with a Christian minister, and nearly two-thirds of these respondents say their opinion of the pastor they know is "very positive" (64%).

As one might expect, these positive views are not evenly distributed across the population, but *all* groups report higher opinions of a pastor personally known to them than of "pastors, priests or other church leaders" as a general category. This broad finding may indicate negative overtones at work broadly within society that influence

THE PROBLEM IS NOT THAT THE AVERAGE AMERICAN HAS A NEGATIVE PERCEPTION OF CHRISTIAN MINISTERS; IT'S THAT THE AVERAGE AMERICAN DOESN'T THINK ABOUT THEM AT ALL

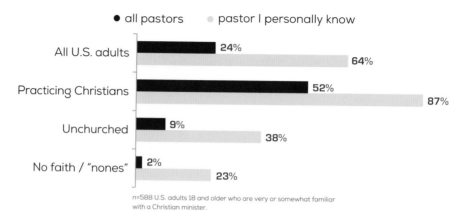

OPINION OF PASTORS, BY FAITH SEGMENT

% "very positive" among U.S. adults who are familiar with a Christian minister

● all pastors   ○ pastor I personally know

All U.S. adults
24%
64%

Practicing Christians
52%
87%

Unchurched
9%
38%

No faith / "nones"
2%
23%

n=588 U.S. adults 18 and older who are very or somewhat familiar
with a Christian minister.

people's views of Christianity, perhaps even without their awareness. For example, 26 percent of the religiously unaffiliated (sometimes called "nones") say they personally know a Christian minister, and one-quarter of those who do have a very positive opinion of him or her (23%)—yet only 2 percent say they have a positive opinion of pastors overall. Similarly, among unchurched adults who personally know a pastor (34%), one-third says they have a very high opinion of the pastor whom they know (38%) but only one in 11 has a high opinion more generally (9%).

On the other hand, practicing Christians—who say their faith is very important in their life and have attended a worship service within the past month—view pastors more warmly, both in general (52%) and specific to the pastor whom they know best (87%).

Of the people who personally know a Christian minister—57 percent of all U.S. adults—four out of five are acquainted with him or her because of current (45%) or past (32%) church involvement. The remaining one in five knows a pastor because they are a relative, a neighbor or a fellow member of a community group or a local nonprofit, or because they share some other social connection.

Since Millennials, the youngest generation of adults, are least likely to attend church, it is no surprise they're more apt to know a pastor through *past* church involvement rather than *current* attendance. Three out of five Elders, on the other hand, are acquainted with a pastor because of current churchgoing, and just one in six because of past attendance.

The generational trends reflected here are indicative of a broader shift when it comes to church involvement. The unchurched made up 30 percent of the U.S. adult population in the 1990s; 33 percent in the 2000s; and 43 percent by 2014. The "unchurched" category includes those who are "de-churched" (33% actively attended at some point but no longer do so) and those who are "purely unchurched" (10% have no previous exposure to church involvement).[24]

HOW PEOPLE KNOW PASTORS, BY GENERATION

% among U.S. adults who are familiar with a Christian minister

● past church involvement ● current church involvement

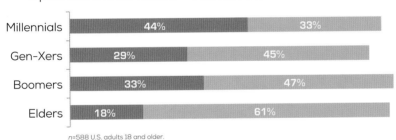

	past church involvement	current church involvement
Millennials	44%	33%
Gen-Xers	29%	45%
Boomers	33%	47%
Elders	18%	61%

n=588 U.S. adults 18 and older.

FURTHER FROM THE CULTURAL CENTER

The national drop off in churchgoing (and in Bible engagement, explored in a later chapter) has contributed to a groundswell of cultural sentiment that Christians are irrelevant and extreme. Barna has found that, for many Americans, the definition of religious extremism extends beyond religiously motivated violence. Three out of five U.S. adults believe it is "religiously extreme" to try to convert someone to your faith (60%); eight out of 10 "nones" say evangelism—one of the central actions of Christian conviction—is extremist (83%). A majority of adults says believing same-sex relationships are morally wrong is extremist (52%). Two out of five say it's extreme to quit a good-paying job to pursue mission work in another country (42%). And, while not majority opinions, millions of people agree that donating regularly to religious causes, reading the Bible silently in public and even volunteering are religiously extreme.[25]

Beyond specific religious activities and attitudes, the perception of Christians' extremism is becoming entrenched among the nation's non-Christians. Forty-five percent of "nones" agree with the statement "Christianity is extremist." *Almost half.*

THE PERCEPTION OF CHRISTIANS' EXTREMISM IS BECOMING ENTRENCHED AMONG THE NATION'S NON-CHRISTIANS

Compounding the impact of these unfriendly views is the fact that practicing Christians make up a shrinking slice of the overall population. In 2001, 43 percent of all U.S. adults qualified as practicing Christians. As of late 2016, just 31 percent met the criteria. And among Millennials the proportion is even smaller: Just one in five is a practicing Christian (21%).

In a separate study of U.S. clergy sponsored by Maclellan Foundation, Barna found that Protestant pastors are aware of the cultural trends away from the "Christian default" of the past. Just one in five believes "a Christian nation" is an accurate description of the U.S. today (20%), while substantial majorities say "a religiously plural nation" (87%), "a nation in transition spiritually" (87%), "a secular nation" (76%) and "a post-Christian nation" (67%) are accurate. Eighty-five percent say they are concerned that "Christians remaining faithful and effective as a minority within the U.S." will affect their ability to minister effectively in the coming decade.

These are just a handful of the trends Barna has been tracking nationally in an effort to understand the Christian community's changing role in and relationship to the dominant culture. They show the Church is being moved to the margins. Pastors—and faithful, practicing lay Christians—are being squeezed from the cultural center.*

---

* For an in-depth look at these trends, check out *Good Faith* by David Kinnaman and Gabe Lyons.

23. INFLUENCE

Do people think pastors are good for their community?

Pastors sense that the weight of their words reaches beyond their pulpit and into the lives of their congregants—and also, at least to some extent, into the public square. But how do people perceive the benefits (or drawbacks) of their influence? And what do pastors think about their standing in the community?

PUBLIC PERCEPTIONS

Just one in five U.S. adults believes Christian ministers are "very influential" in their community (19%). One-quarter says pastors' influence is minimal (24% not very + not at all influential), while a lukewarm plurality says they are "somewhat influential" (40%). Not surprisingly, church leaders' more captive audiences—such as practicing Christians (44%), evangelicals (42%) and weekly churchgoers (37%)—are more apt to esteem them as very influential.

Those of no faith—a group that includes atheists, agnostics and "nones"—are most likely to believe pastors hold negligible local influence (44%), but the findings suggest this view may have more to do with indifference than disdain: One-third of the religiously unaffiliated admits they are simply "not sure" whether clergy play an influential role in their community (33%)—twice the national average (17%).

It's one thing to ask if church leaders wield great influence; Barna also wanted to know, is their influence good? Do Christian ministers have a positive or negative reputation in their cities and neighborhoods?

Four in 10 U.S. adults assert the presence of pastors is "a significant benefit" to their community (40%) and one in four says it's "a small benefit" (26%)—combined, that's two-thirds of the overall population who believe pastors benefit their neighborhood. In a sign of stiffer headwinds in the decades to come, however, Millennials are less inclined than older Americans to say pastors are a significant benefit (29%),

> TWO-THIRDS OF THE OVERALL POPULATION BELIEVES PASTORS BENEFIT THEIR NEIGHBORHOOD

especially when compared to Elders, who tend to be quite convinced of the significant benefits pastors bring to their city or town (60%).

A small minority of U.S. adults feels that ministers pose a disadvantage to their community (5%). As one might predict, this view is concentrated among adults with no religious faith (12% small + significant disadvantage) or who identify with a religion other than Christianity (9%). Again, however, a majority of both groups is more likely to feel neutral on the question than to be actively negative: One-third of those with no faith and one-quarter of adherents to another faith judge pastors to be "neither a benefit nor a disadvantage," and one in four among both groups is just not sure.

U.S. ADULTS ON THE BENEFIT OR DISADVANTAGE OF PASTORS' PRESENCE IN THEIR COMMUNITY

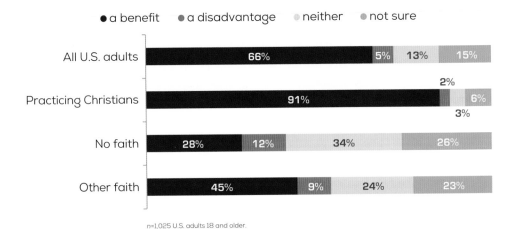

● a benefit   ● a disadvantage   ○ neither   ● not sure

	a benefit	a disadvantage	neither	not sure
All U.S. adults	66%	5%	13%	15%
Practicing Christians	91%	2%	6%	3%
No faith	28%	12%	34%	26%
Other faith	45%	9%	24%	23%

n=1,025 U.S. adults 18 and older.

PASTORS' PERCEPTIONS

The public's neutral or noncommittal responses concerning ministers' influence are reflected in pastors' perceptions of their place within community life. When asked how satisfied they are with the respect pastors are afforded by their surrounding community, about one in five says it's "excellent" (22%). Just about half say it is "good" (48%) and another one in five rates community respect for clergy as "average" (21%). These somewhat bland responses corroborate the general population's indifference.

Black pastors are more likely than white leaders to be satisfied with the respect they receive from their community (41% vs. 21%). This lends support to Terry Linhart's contention that historically black churches often excel at esteeming and honoring their pastors, which can help those church leaders sustain their confidence in their call to ministry. (See pp. 89 for Linhart's Q&A with Barna.)

As we saw in Part I, pastors who earn less than $40,000 a year have a counterintuitive tendency to report higher levels of satisfaction on many measures—and they are no different on the question of respect they receive from their surrounding community. The lowest-paid pastors are twice as likely as those who earn between $40,000 and $60,000 annually to rate their satisfaction as "excellent" (31% vs. 16%), and 11 points more likely to do so than those who earn more than $60,000 (20%).

As expected, pastors who are very satisfied with their vocation or ministry in their current church are far more likely than those who are less satisfied to report high levels of respect from their community.

In the Maclellan study of U.S. clergy mentioned previously, Barna found that, even in their own congregations, pastors feel their influence is limited. Only one-third says they have "a lot" of influence on how members of their church think about current issues in society (33%); most say they have "some" (60%). This limited influence may be to the good, since only about one in three church leaders says they are "very prepared" to teach their congregation how to engage in constructive conversations with people who disagree with them on sensitive social issues (37%).[26]

EVEN IN THEIR OWN CONGREGATIONS, PASTORS FEEL THEIR INFLUENCE IS LIMITED

Dallas Willard wrote, "The task of Christian pastors and leaders is to present Christ's answers to the basic questions of life and to bring those answers forward as knowledge—primarily to those who are seeking and are open to following him, but also to all who happen to hear."[27] It appears that many pastors do not feel equal to this task. What must be done to equip and encourage them?

WHO TRUSTS PASTORS MOST—AND LEAST?

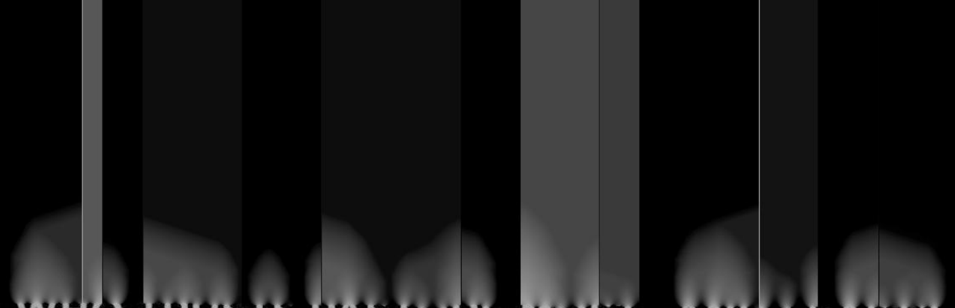

Faith practice, political ideology and stage of life affect how people esteem the wisdom of pastors and priests. But factors like education, income, gender, ethnicity and socioeconomic status generally have less sway on Americans' perception of pastoral insight.

"I believe Christian ministers are ***very credible*** when it comes to important issues of our day."

ALL U.S. ADULTS: 21%

- EVANGELICALS: 52%
- PRACTICING CHRISTIANS: 51%
- ACTIVE CHURCHGOERS: 45%
- BORN AGAIN: 36%
- POLITICAL CONSERVATIVES: 34%
- PARENTS: 30%
- SELF-IDENTIFIED CHRISTIANS: 26%
- MARRIED ADULTS: 24%

"I believe Christian ministers are ***not at all credible*** when it comes to important issues of our day."

ALL U.S. ADULTS: 11%

- NO FAITH/ "NONES": 39%
- NEVER CHURCHED: 36%
- DO NOT IDENTIFY AS CHRISTIAN: 33%
- POLITICAL LIBERALS: 20%
- NOT BORN AGAIN: 16%
- SINGLE ADULTS: 14%
- DECHURCHED: 13%
- ADULTS WITHOUT KIDS: 13%

People are more likely to welcome pastors' voices when it involves spiritual matters, such as God's will or the church. Trust in pastors wanes, however, when it comes to politics and justice. Here's how Americans rate the reliability of pastors and priests on a key topics.

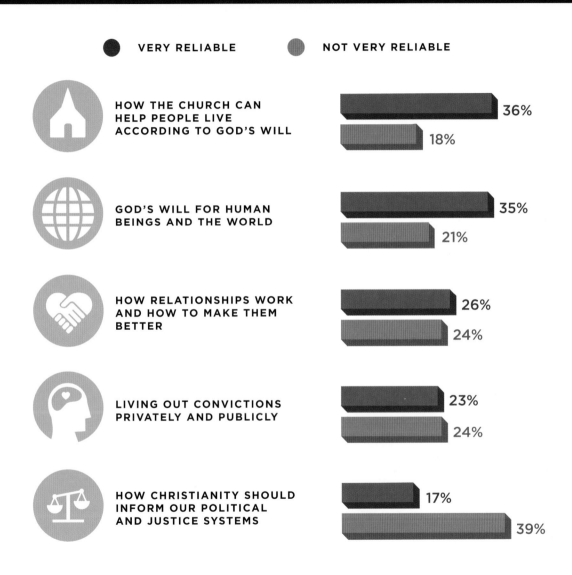

● VERY RELIABLE   ● NOT VERY RELIABLE

HOW THE CHURCH CAN HELP PEOPLE LIVE ACCORDING TO GOD'S WILL
36%
18%

GOD'S WILL FOR HUMAN BEINGS AND THE WORLD
35%
21%

HOW RELATIONSHIPS WORK AND HOW TO MAKE THEM BETTER
26%
24%

LIVING OUT CONVICTIONS PRIVATELY AND PUBLICLY
23%
24%

HOW CHRISTIANITY SHOULD INFORM OUR POLITICAL AND JUSTICE SYSTEMS
17%
39%

Do people believe pastors are reliable guides for life?

Despite how influential they feel (or do not feel), pastors play a unique role in the lives of their congregants. Their sermons and personal counsel inform decisions and attitudes about everything from God's forgiveness to the Bible, from family relationships to politics. And their influence shows: The majority of practicing Christians says pastors are a "very credible" source of wisdom "when it comes to the most important issues of our day" (51%).

But what about the broader population? Does the average American appreciate the wisdom Christian ministers bring to the public square?

One in five U.S. adults believes that pastors are a very credible source of insight on today's issues (21%). One in four thinks pastors are "not very" (14%) or "not at all credible" (11%), and 15 percent are "not sure." But the plurality of Americans once again occupies a kind of noncommittal, mushy middle: Two in five say pastors are a "somewhat credible" source of wisdom (39%).

Pastors' perceived wisdom rises and falls according to topic. More to the point, people seem to trust pastors when it comes to overtly "spiritual" topics, but are less confident in their counsel

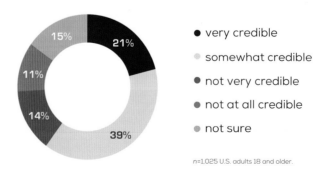

PASTORS' CREDIBILITY ON THE IMPORTANT ISSUES OF OUR DAY

% among U.S. adults

- very credible
- somewhat credible
- not very credible
- not at all credible
- not sure

15% 21% 11% 14% 39%

n=1,025 U.S. adults 18 and older.

PASTORS' RELIABILITY ON SPECIFIC ISSUES, BY FAITH PRACTICE

% "very reliable" among U.S. adults

● all U.S. adults   ● practicing Christians   ○ non-practicing Christians   ● no faith

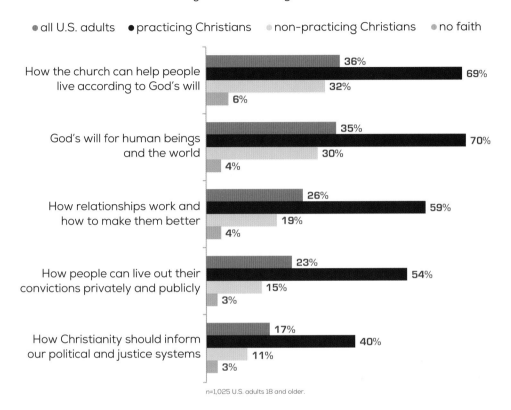

How the church can help people live according to God's will
- 36%
- 69%
- 32%
- 6%

God's will for human beings and the world
- 35%
- 70%
- 30%
- 4%

How relationships work and how to make them better
- 26%
- 59%
- 19%
- 4%

How people can live out their convictions privately and publicly
- 23%
- 54%
- 15%
- 3%

How Christianity should inform our political and justice systems
- 17%
- 40%
- 11%
- 3%

n=1,025 U.S. adults 18 and older.

on more everyday, "close-to-the-ground" issues. For instance, one-third of all adults consider Christian ministers very reliable sources of information and counsel when it comes to "how the church can help people live according to God's will" (36%) and "God's will for human beings and the world" (35%). Fewer believe pastors are very reliable, however, when it comes to "how relationships work and how to make them better" (26%) and "how people can live out their convictions privately and publicly" (23%).

People are most skeptical about pastors' insights when it comes to "how Christianity should inform our political and justice systems." Just one out of eight adults believes pastoral wisdom on

PEOPLE SEEM TO TRUST PASTORS WHEN IT COMES TO OVERTLY "SPIRITUAL" TOPICS, BUT ARE LESS CONFIDENT IN THEIR COUNSEL ON MORE EVERYDAY ISSUES

this topic is very reliable (17%), half the number of those who say pastors are not very (20%) or not at all reliable (19%). And even though practicing Christians are among the most convinced of pastors' wisdom on applying faith to the political realm, fewer than half say ministers are very reliable in this regard (40%). This complements the results of Barna election polling among U.S. voters, which found that pastors rank quite low on a list of voter influences, below religious beliefs (which top the list), family members, news media and friends.[28]

LOSS OF AUTHORITY

In the Maclellan study of U.S. clergy, pastors were asked if it is harder, easier or about the same today as five years ago to speak out on moral and social issues. A plurality of Protestant leaders says it's about the same (48%), but nearly as many say speaking out is harder (44%). Reasons they offer for believing it's more difficult include the growing sentiment that Christians are intolerant, the complex relational and political issues surrounding homosexuality and traditional sexual ethics, and the loss of the Bible as a cultural source of moral authority.

These feelings are certainly supported by the data. For example, through ongoing research for American Bible Society, Barna has tracked a decrease from generation to generation of people who trust the authority of the Scriptures because "the Bible contains everything a person needs to know to live a meaningful life." Among Elders in the U.S., eight out of 10 believe the Bible is authoritative (79%), and the ratio of those who are engaged with the Bible (26%) to those who are skeptical (13%) is 2:1.* Among Millennials, fewer than six in 10 believe the Bible is authoritative (56%), and the ratio of Bible engagement (12%) to skepticism (26%) is 1:2. Non-Christian Millennials are also much more likely than Elders to say the Bible is "just a story" (50%), "mythology" (38%) or "a fairy tale" (30%).[29]

BARNA HAS TRACKED A DECREASING PERCENTAGE FROM GENERATION TO GENERATION OF PEOPLE WHO TRUST THE AUTHORITY OF THE BIBLE

---

* For Bible engagement definitions, see Appendix B. Definitions.

Skepticism of the Bible's authority is one aspect of Millennials' mistrust of institutions more generally. In research for the Association for Biblical Higher Education (ABHE), Barna interviewed Christian educators who see this institutional alienation in their students. One professor said, "They have moved from a truth culture, whereby the facts of the matter were the primary consideration in adult conversation, to a therapy culture, whereby their first question is how it makes them or others feel." Such a "post-truth" culture inevitably makes communicating God's truth a challenging endeavor. What adaptive tools do pastors need to accomplish their mission within a culture of complexity? And where can they find those tools?

25. TRAITS

What are the qualities of a good pastor?

With varying degrees of authority, pastors act as role models not only for their congregation, but also for the community where they live and minister. But what are the essential virtues of an effective church leader?

From a list of available options, a plurality of both U.S. adults and pastors choose "love for people, desire to help people" as one of the top two qualities of an effective church leader. However, the general public holds this virtue in higher regard than pastors: About half of all Americans prioritize this trait, compared to three in 10 pastors. Significant minorities in each group say "love of God / Jesus" is one of the top two traits a church leader needs to be effective. Thus, the twin virtues of loving God and loving others—the two greatest commandments—are elevated by both pastors and the American public as essential pastoral qualities. Beyond these two attributes, however, the groups begin to differ significantly.

To researchers' surprise, a slight majority of pastors opted to ignore the list of 11 options and selected "other" as one of their two possible choices (54%), which likely indicates that individual pastors have uniquely specific ideas about what virtues make for effective church leadership. Given an opportunity to write in, pastors offer a wide variety of traits they believe are essential for their work. The most common themes that emerge from their answers include humility, consistent spiritual disciplines (especially prayer), patience, compassion, flexibility, integrity, a clear ministry calling, and good communication and listening skills.

Among the pastors who selected from the survey options, "zeal, passion, commitment" and "leadership, vision" are about equally popular—but the general public does not consider these traits as essential as "insight, wisdom, discernment." U.S. adults

THE TWIN VIRTUES OF LOVING GOD AND LOVING OTHERS ARE ELEVATED BY BOTH PASTORS AND THE AMERICAN PUBLIC AS ESSENTIAL PASTORAL QUALITIES

TOP TRAITS OF A GOOD PASTOR:
PASTORS VS. U.S. ADULTS

RANK	PASTORS	ALL U.S. ADULTS
1	Other (54%)	Love for people, desire to help people (48%)
2	Love for people, desire to help people (30%)	Love of God / Jesus (33%)
3	Love of God / Jesus (21%)	Insight, wisdom, discernment (22%)
4	Zeal, passion, commitment (17%)	Bible knowledge (15%)
5	Leadership, vision (16%)	Faithfulness, obedience (14%)
6	Faithfulness, obedience (10%)	Cultural understanding (13%)
7	Insight, wisdom, discernment (9%)	Leadership, vision (13%)
8	Bible knowledge (5%)	Zeal, passion, commitment (7%)
9	Team leadership (4%)	Theological knowledge (6%)
10	Cultural understanding (4%)	Team leadership (5%)
11	Theological knowledge (2%)	Strategic thinking (3%)
12	Strategic thinking (2%)	Other (3%)

n=527 U.S. pastors, *n*=1,025 U.S. adults 18 and older; "don't know" was also an option.

are more apt than pastors to consider "Bible knowledge" and "cultural understanding" as top qualities of an effective church leader. Few in either group highly prioritize "theological knowledge."

It's interesting to consider these findings in light of the fact that just 9 percent of all pastors say seminaries are doing "very well" at preparing pastors to effectively lead churches today. Many theological institutions emphasize knowledge acquisition over interpersonal skill development, increasing leadership aptitude and spiritual maturity—yet pastors' write-in answers on the top traits essential for effective church leadership make it clear that most believe character is more vital than intellect.

26. VOCATION

How does a non-ministry career compare with a pastoral calling?

In Christian tradition, the words "vocation" and "calling" encompass much more than a career in full-time ministry; they apply to all types of work outside the walls of the church.[30] But according to most U.S. adults—especially (and paradoxically) practicing Christians—pastors' work is more important than their own career or vocation.

Half of all working Americans say church work is "much more" (28%) or "a little more" (22%) important than their career choice. One in five says a pastoral vocation is of equal importance with their career (20%), and one in six believes their own vocation is more important than a Christian minister's (18%). Exceptionally inclined to believe their career is more important than pastoring are Millennials (31%) and those who are religiously unaffiliated ("nones," 47%).

In contrast, three-quarters of practicing Christians say a pastor's vocation is more important than their own (51% much more, 22% a little more). The root of this belief appears to be

HOW CHURCH WORK COMPARES TO RESPONDENT'S CAREER

% among currently employed or retired U.S. adults

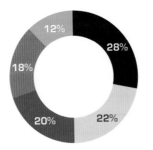

- much more important
- a little more important
- of equal importance
- not as important
- not sure

12%
28%
22%
20%
18%

n=747 adults 18 and older.

theological or philosophical, not practical. That is, the vast majority of practicing Christians would recommend their career / vocation to a young person who is considering it (40% definitely, 41% probably), so it seems likely their view of church work reflects reverence for ministry calling rather than rejection of their own vocational choices. Still, the data suggests the sacred-secular divide is alive and well among most practicing Christians today.

A majority of adults would encourage a young person to pursue a career in their field (29% definitely, 41% probably), but several factors, in addition to Christian practice, impact a person's inclination to do so. Among these are ethnicity or race, educational attainment and—not surprisingly—annual income. U.S. adults who earn a salary of $100,000 or more or have completed at least some college are more likely than those who make less than $50,000 or went to high school only to say they would "definitely" recommend their career. Black and Hispanic Americans are also more apt than white adults to definitely recommend their vocation.

Pastors are twice as likely as U.S. adults to say they would "definitely" encourage someone who is considering a career as a pastor to pursue it (63%)—that is, to recommend their vocation to a young person. As in the general population, pastors of color are more inclined than white pastors to say they would definitely encourage a young person to consider a career in church ministry. But unlike the income and educational trends among U.S. adults, lower-paid leaders and those who did *not* attend seminary are just as inclined, statistically speaking, as their top-earning and more-educated colleagues to recommend their vocation.

For pastors, earning potential appears to have less of an effect than their church's size and the trajectory of its growth. Leaders of large and / or growing congregations are more apt to say they'd definitely recommend their vocation, compared to leaders of small churches and those whose attendance has been flat over the past year.

THE DATA SUGGESTS THE SACRED-SECULAR DIVIDE IS ALIVE AND WELL AMONG MOST PRACTICING CHRISTIANS TODAY

A pastor's satisfaction with their work, however, has an even greater impact on their willingness to recommend a pastoral vocation. A majority of less-satisfied leaders—larger than the majority among all U.S. adults—says they would, in fact, encourage a young person to pursue a ministry career. But they are less likely than the norm among pastors to say they would *definitely* do so, and nearly twice as likely to say they would *not* recommend a career in church ministry (15% vs. 8% among all pastors).

Significant for the future health of the U.S. church, most pastors—even those who are not very satisfied in their work—believe what they do is worth it and would encourage up-and-coming leaders to take a similar path. That's good news! However, there seems to be growing ambivalence among the wider population about whether pastoral work is important—

WOULD ENCOURAGE A YOUNG PERSON TO PURSUE A CAREER IN RESPONDENT'S VOCATIONAL FIELD: PASTORS VS. U.S. ADULTS

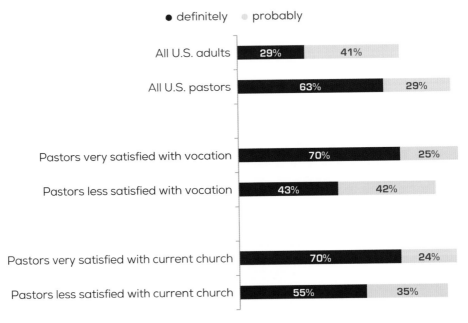

● definitely ○ probably

	definitely	probably
All U.S. adults	29%	41%
All U.S. pastors	63%	29%
Pastors very satisfied with vocation	70%	25%
Pastors less satisfied with vocation	43%	42%
Pastors very satisfied with current church	70%	24%
Pastors less satisfied with current church	55%	35%

n=887 U.S. Protestant pastors; n=747 U.S. adults.

particularly among Millennials, a surprising number of whom say their own work is more important than church ministry. Barna has found in previous research that Millennials are keener than older generations to integrate their personal values into their career, and are more inclined toward risk and entrepreneurship—especially if their business idea can be connected to social good. These and other factors may contribute to the sense among today's pastors, explored in "Mentoring" (see page 86), that identifying future church leaders is becoming a more complex task.

THERE SEEMS TO BE GROWING AMBIVALENCE AMONG THE WIDER POPULATION ABOUT WHETHER PASTORAL WORK IS IMPORTANT

27. RECONCILIATION

How do pastors view their church's role in racial justice?

Race is certainly one factor of cultural complexity that impacts both the life of the nation and the life of the Church. When it comes to race relations, most U.S. pastors agree with the wider population that there are real obstacles to surmount and considerable work ahead in order to accomplish true and lasting reconciliation. However, while the general public's views on these matters tend to be divided along racial and generational lines, pastors' views, for the most part, are not. For Protestant pastors in America, one's theological tradition is a stronger consideration than one's racial identity or shared peer assumptions. Mainline pastors under 50, for example, have more opinions on race issues in common with their older mainline colleagues than with their non-mainline age cohort, and the same is true for non-mainline leaders under 50: They are more similar to their older colleagues than to younger mainline pastors.

There is strong consensus among U.S. adults (84%) and pastors (86%) that "there is a lot of anger and hostility between different ethnic and racial groups in America today." Pastors tend to agree regardless of their denominational affiliation; Americans overall agree without respect to their race or generation.

Moreover, two-thirds of pastors and U.S. adults agree that "people of color are often put at a disadvantage because of their race." When these majorities are segmented into various population groups, however, agreement is not equally widespread. Race / ethnicity (77% all non-white vs. 62% white) and generation (73% Millennials vs. 62% Boomers, for example) are predictors of how likely an American is to agree—yet they are not robust predictors among U.S. pastors. Much more significant are denominational differences: Mainline Protestant leaders are far more apt than non-mainline pastors to agree there are social disadvantages for people of color in the United States.

The persistent mainline / non-mainline split on race has its roots in the Civil Rights movement. In his book *Getting Religion*, longtime religion editor for *Newsweek* Kenneth L. Woodward charts the movement of Northern mainline (mostly white) clergy toward alignment with Martin Luther King, Jr., which reached its apex at Selma. "After Selma," Woodward writes, "veterans of the march would talk of their experience as life changing. It wasn't just a memorable moment: it was also a moral credential. . . . Thereafter, where one stood on the issue of public agitation on behalf of civil rights became for activist clergy the measure of authentic faith."[31] In short, a commitment to racial justice is, for many mainline Protestants, a fundamental feature of Christian identity.

A COMMITMENT TO RACIAL JUSTICE IS, FOR MANY MAINLINE PROTESTANTS, A FUNDAMENTAL FEATURE OF CHRISTIAN IDENTITY

These differences can also be seen on other statements related to race in America. Nine out of 10 mainline ministers agree that "law enforcement and the judicial system treat people of color and white people differently," but fewer than six in 10 non-mainline pastors concur—still a majority, but a significantly smaller one. And two-thirds of mainline leaders believe "the 'Black Lives Matter' movement is an appropriate response to the problem of police violence against black citizens," compared to just one in five non-mainline leaders.

Pastors and the general public are aligned overall on their assessment of race relations, but Christian ministers are harsher than U.S. adults when it comes to the church's role in perpetuating racism. Roughly one-third of Americans agrees that "Christian churches are part of the problem when it comes to racism," a smaller percentage than among pastors. Mainline leaders are especially critical of U.S. churches in this regard, but close to half of non-mainline church leaders also agree—still more than among the general population.

RACE IN AMERICA: MAINLINE AND NON-MAINLINE PASTORS VS. U.S. ADULTS

% "agree" among U.S. pastors and U.S. adults 18 and older

● all U.S. adults   ● mainline pastors   ● non-mainline pastors

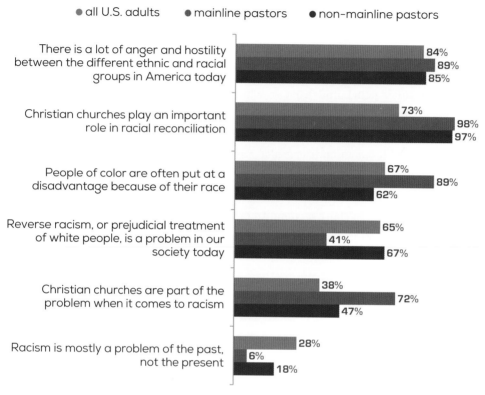

There is a lot of anger and hostility between the different ethnic and racial groups in America today
- 84%
- 89%
- 85%

Christian churches play an important role in racial reconciliation
- 73%
- 98%
- 97%

People of color are often put at a disadvantage because of their race
- 67%
- 89%
- 62%

Reverse racism, or prejudicial treatment of white people, is a problem in our society today
- 65%
- 41%
- 67%

Christian churches are part of the problem when it comes to racism
- 38%
- 72%
- 47%

Racism is mostly a problem of the past, not the present
- 28%
- 6%
- 18%

n=600 U.S. Protestant pastors; n=1,237 U.S. adults 18 and older.

However disapproving pastors may be about the church's past contributions to racism, they are also quite hopeful about the impact churches can make on the future—and U.S. adults share that hope. Virtually all pastors, both mainline and non-mainline, agree that "Christian churches play an important role in racial reconciliation." Three-quarters of all Americans, both black and white, also believe local congregations can and should play a part in reconciliation.

What churches are making an effort to do so? Half of all pastors say "racial justice and reconciliation is among my church's top 10 priorities" (51%). On this statement, mainline and non-mainline pastors are equally likely to agree, but there is a difference between white pastors (50% agree) and pastors of color (61%). Barna asked all pastors who agree with the statement where racial justice ranks on a list of their church's top 10 priorities, and found that leaders of color (70%) are more likely than white pastors (50%) to rank it among their congregation's top five concerns.

PASTORS ARE QUITE HOPEFUL ABOUT THE IMPACT CHURCHES CAN MAKE ON THE FUTURE— AND U.S. ADULTS SHARE THAT HOPE

Q&A WITH DAVID BAILEY

DAVID BAILEY

David M. Bailey is the founder and executive director of Arrabon, a ministry that equips churches and organizations to engage in the ministry of reconciliation with cultural intelligence. He is an active speaker, consultant and strategist for many national organizations on cultural intelligence and culture-making. David was named by *Christianity Today* as one of "The 20 Most Creative Christians We Know" and is the executive producer of the Urban Doxology Project. His greatest honor in life is to be married to his wonderful and beautiful wife, Joy.

Q: An overwhelming 98 percent of pastors believe churches play an important role in racial reconciliation, yet only half say it is among their own church's top 10 priorities. Why is there a disconnect between awareness of the problem and participation in the solution?

A: We must acknowledge our history and understand how it has caused the problems we face today, even though doing so is deeply uncomfortable. We should never "get over it" by forgetting. Rather, we should remember and then confess wrongdoing and its consequences, and repent. Repentance is more than saying "I'm sorry"; it means doing something about it.

Where to start? Missionaries often know they are going to "cross a culture," so they take time to understand the sociology and anthropology of the new people they will engage with. Pastors working domestically don't often engage this same practice, so generally they don't lead their church with strong cross-cultural intelligence. As a result, too many Christians jump into conversations about racial reconciliation without a firm foundation of cultural understanding.

We need that foundation, and we need a biblical understanding of what it means to be human. For example, if we interpret the Great Commission as "saving souls," our interactions with people inevitably contain some level of dehumanization because we have a disembodied anthropology. But if the Great Commission is about "making disciples of all the nations," then we see disciples as whole people with bodies, souls and a place of origin. We see that discipleship is comprehensive. The Bible has a holistic understanding of humanity in which the spirit, soul and body are part of God's redemption, reconciliation and restoration.

Q: If you were to coach a white pastor on how to talk to their congregation about reconciliation, what is most important for them to know?

A: As I mentioned, most people don't have the theological, historical or sociological tools to deal with this heavy topic. It's like teaching calculus to a fifth grader without giving them the proper preparation and time to mature. So here are the things I recommend to a white pastor to prepare and mature their congregation to be ministers of reconciliation in this area.

- **Be committed and intentional.** Nothing gets done right without investing time and money, and in relationships. Too often pastors try to get this work done without a cost. If a pastor is not willing to invest, it would be better for them not to start. After hearing just one sermon or even a sermon series, people revert to the status quo.
- **Go on your own journey.** My grandmother has a saying: "You can't come from where you've never been." As a white pastor, commit yourself to be in a space of displacement indefinitely. Join some type of ethnic minority social club or gathering. Go by yourself and be a part of that community for nine months to a year so you can know what it is like to be a minority in a community.
- **Get organizational consulting and training from experts.** Too often, predominantly white organizations ask the minorities who are already part of the organization to help them reform. This is a bad idea. The person who is a minority in your organization already has two jobs: the job on their job description and the job of representing their race or ethnicity. If that person is a woman, she has a third job representing her gender. Adding the role of race expert or organizational change manager is too much. Invite a qualified person or organization to help you through the process.

Q: Why is worship often a sticking point in pursuit of a cross-cultural embodiment of the Church?

A: Often when a church tries to adopt a cross-cultural embodiment of worship, people who aren't used to living a cross-cultural life experience discomfort and want to put on the brakes. If what attracted them to the church was comfortable spirituality, they may leave. (If they don't leave, they might complain to the point where the leaders hope they leave!)

Worship is not only expressive, but also formational. As leaders, we have to ask ourselves, How are we forming people? Are we forming people in consumer spirituality? Are we forming people to prefer others before themselves? Are we creating a church for the least of these or for our big givers? When we ask ourselves these questions with honesty and transparency, we allow space for the Holy Spirit to speak to us through a diverse group of brothers and sisters and hear things we wouldn't normally hear. When we don't ask these questions, we leave ourselves open to malformation according to our own cultural blind spots.

28. FREEDOM

How concerned are pastors about religious liberty?

The past several years are notable for the number of events that raise questions about religious freedom in the United States. These include, among many others, the Supreme Court's ruling in *Obergefell v. Hodges* requiring all 50 states to issue marriage licenses to same-sex couples; the jailing of Rowan County, Kentucky, Clerk Kim Davis for refusing to do so; continuing adjudication of the Obamacare requirement that employers, including faith-based organizations, provide birth control to their employees; the activist clashes over passage of Indiana's Religious Freedom Restoration Act; and the U.S. Department of Education's directive that all public schools must allow students to use facilities that correspond to their gender identity, rather than to their birth sex.

These and other issues are heightening the sense among many Americans—including pastors—that religious liberty may be under threat. In the nationwide study of U.S. clergy conducted in partnership with Maclellan Foundation, Barna found that non-mainline Protestant pastors tend to express more concern than mainline ministers. But a majority of both groups says they are at least somewhat concerned "that religious freedom will become more restricted in the next five years in the U.S."

The specifics of church leaders' concerns for the future vary, and not all are directly related to religious freedom. With differing levels of intensity, pastors agree it's likely in the next 10 years that society will become less moral; that Christians will have less influence in society; that freedoms other than religious liberty will be put at risk; and that citizens' ability to freely practice their faith will be diminished.

A MAJORITY OF PASTORS IS AT LEAST SOMEWHAT CONCERNED THAT RELIGIOUS FREEDOM WILL BECOME MORE RESTRICTED IN THE NEXT FIVE YEARS

CONCERNS ABOUT FUTURE RESTRICTIONS ON RELIGIOUS LIBERTY

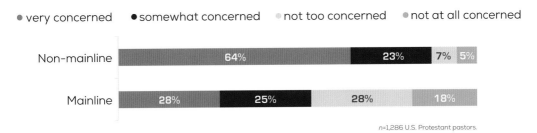

● very concerned ● somewhat concerned ● not too concerned ● not at all concerned

Non-mainline	64%	23%	7%	5%
Mainline	28%	25%	28%	18%

n=1,286 U.S. Protestant pastors.

THE LIKELIHOOD OF OUTCOMES IN THE NEXT 10 YEARS
% "very" + "somewhat likely" among U.S. Protestant pastors

Outcome	% Non-Mainline	% Mainline
Society in general will be less moral	95	73
Christians / people of faith will have less influence in society	88	86
Other kinds of freedoms, not just religious, will also be at risk	89	75
The government will have too much control over religious institutions	80	47
People will have less ability to practice their faith without interference	77	51
People will be more free to live according to their conscience	51	62

n=600 U.S. Protestant pastors.

When asked to assess the current state of religious freedom in the U.S., non-mainline leaders are much more likely to express pessimism—85 percent overall say it is becoming less valued—than mainline pastors (54%). Yet, a majority among mainline leaders also believes First-Amendment freedoms are becoming less valued by the broader culture.

SOCIETY'S VALUE OF RELIGIOUS LIBERTY

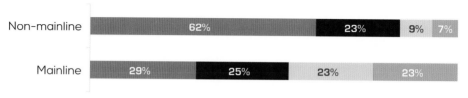

- ● definitely becoming less valued   ● somewhat alive and well
- ● somewhat becoming less valued   ● definitely alive and well

Non-mainline	62%	23%	9% 7%
Mainline	29%	25%	23% 23%

n=1,286 U.S. Protestant pastors.

A majority of pastors believes the potential impact of declining freedom will have a negative impact on their faith community. And even more than their white counterparts, black pastors say such declines would have a very negative impact (48%). Yet according to a significant minority of pastors, the outcome for Christians won't necessarily be negative. In fact, three in 10 pastors say the impact on the Christian community will be somewhat or even very positive (31%). This minority may see in these challenges an opportunity for the U.S. church to refocus on its mission.

Complete research findings on the ministry issues surrounding religious freedom, along with Barna insights and analysis, will

IMPACT OF DIMINISHED FREEDOM ON THE FAITH COMMUNITY

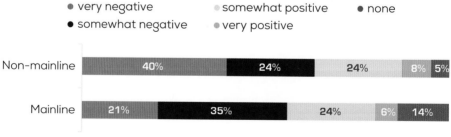

- ● very negative   ● somewhat positive   ● none
- ● somewhat negative   ● very positive

Non-mainline	40%	24%	24%	8% 5%
Mainline	21%	35%	24%	6% 14%

n=1,286 U.S. Protestant pastors.

appear in the forthcoming report *Faith Leaders on Religious Liberty* (Barna Group, 2017). Key findings include:

1. Religious freedom is widely defined as freedom to practice religion without interference from the government.

2. Clergy of all traditions agree that the U.S. is a religiously plural nation and a nation in transition spiritually.

3. Many faith leaders struggle to embrace a form of religious liberty that goes beyond mere self-interest. This is true for all groups in the study; each tends to concern itself with its own interests.

4. Many clergy are finding it increasingly difficult to talk about sensitive cultural topics. Their hesitation is largely due to concerns about how people in the pews will react to such discussions.

5. Clergy often have a one-size-fits-all solution to addressing issues: sermons. This is not necessarily bad, but it does reflect a lack of other tools to disciple and guide congregants' thinking.

6. Especially for non-mainline pastors, religious liberty and LGBT issues are inextricably linked. There is tremendous angst about how to move forward.

7. Mainline and non-Christian leaders hold many similar views on these matters, while non-mainline and Catholics pastors tend to share similar perspectives.

8. Most faith leaders believe their congregants want help addressing issues of religious liberty and complex questions that arise in a pluralistic culture—and they view their role as unique and important.

29. OPPORTUNITIES

What do people want from pastors?

Given people's inclination to trust the wisdom of pastors more on "spiritual" issues than on concerns that touch everyday life, it's not a surprise that overtly Christian themes head the list of teaching topics people say would be most valuable to them. (Respondents could choose up to two options.) One in four says they are personally interested in "Christian morals / biblical values (for example, sexual ethics, caring for the poor, care for creation, honesty / integrity, sacrificial giving, serving others)" and one in five expresses interest in "the gospel (Jesus' death and resurrection, how to follow Jesus, God's redemption of the world)" or "how to read / interpret / understand the Bible."

As we saw in "Wisdom" (see pp. 122) a minority of Americans believes pastors are trustworthy guides not only on spiritual matters but also when it comes to human relationships. About one in five says they are hungry to learn more from pastors on "family issues (for example, marriage, parenting, caring for aging parents, divorce, family estrangement, reconciliation)." On the other hand, only 8 percent of adults are interested in hearing pastoral teaching on "social / political issues (for example, same-sex marriage / LGBT rights, abortion, gun rights, tax policy, climate change, drug policy, religious freedom)," which is commensurate with the much smaller percentage of Americans who say pastors are very reliable sources of insight on how faith should inform politics.

More practicing Christians and active churchgoers express a desire to learn about explicitly Christian topics compared to the national norm. For example, practicing Christians are more likely than average to say they'd like to receive pastoral teaching on the gospel, on "who Jesus was or is / who God is / what God is like (God's character)" and on "spiritual disciplines (for example, prayer, meditation, Bible study, fasting, silence / solitude, serving, worship)." But in

MOST VALUABLE PASTORAL TEACHING TOPICS
% among U.S. adults

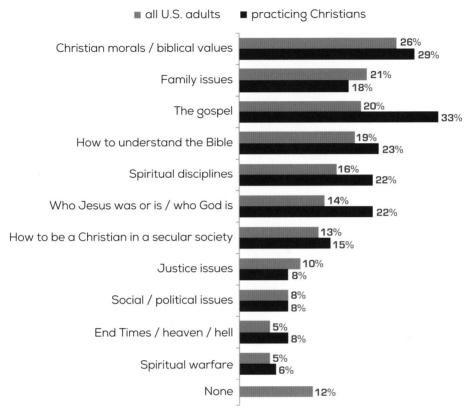

■ all U.S. adults ■ practicing Christians

Topic	all U.S. adults	practicing Christians
Christian morals / biblical values	26%	29%
Family issues	21%	18%
The gospel	20%	33%
How to understand the Bible	19%	23%
Spiritual disciplines	16%	22%
Who Jesus was or is / who God is	14%	22%
How to be a Christian in a secular society	13%	15%
Justice issues	10%	8%
Social / political issues	8%	8%
End Times / heaven / hell	5%	8%
Spiritual warfare	5%	6%
None	12%	

n=1,025 U.S. adults 18 and older; respondents could select up to two options.

addition to the differences between active Christians and other faith groups, including those with no religious affiliation—who are, not surprisingly, less interested overall in hearing from pastors on any topic—there are also some notable differences among the generations.

As a case in point, Millennials are more likely than Boomers to say they would value teaching on "justice issues (for example, racism, gender inequality, capital punishment, immigration, income inequality, prison reform)" and less likely to express interest

DATA DEMONSTRATE WIDESPREAD RELIGIOUS INTEREST AMONG BOTH BELIEVERS AND EVERYDAY AMERICANS

in a pastor's teaching on the gospel or on "how to be a Christian in secular society / in America." Unexpectedly, young adults also are more inclined to want teaching on "spiritual warfare (for example, demonic / Satanic influence, intercessory prayer, charismatic gifts such as speaking in tongues, healing, miracles, prophecy)." They are also most likely among all adults to say "none" of the possible topics would be valuable to them.

In the study on Christian higher education for ABHE mentioned previously, researchers asked U.S. adults what type of religious or faith-based education (if any) they would be most interested in. Only one in three Americans says they are not

U.S. ADULTS' INTERESTS IN FAITH-BASED EDUCATION
% among U.S. adults

● all U.S. adults   ● practicing Christians

	all U.S. adults	practicing Christians
Continued professional development that focuses on integrating faith and applying it to my career	17%	31%
An undergraduate degree for a new career or discipline, with integrated theological training	13%	20%
Single, one-off intensives, refreshers or workshops on a religious topic for personal enrichment	11%	16%
A postgraduate degree that focuses on a new career field or discipline, with integrated theological training	9%	16%
Engagement in a religious education hub in my area where I can study theology for personal enrichment	8%	13%
A postgraduate degree in religion, theology, ministry or biblical studies	6%	12%
A non-degree certification in religious or theological studies	6%	12%
An undergraduate degree in religion, theology, ministry or biblical studies	6%	11%

n=1,000 U.S. adults 18 and older; respondents could select up to three options

interested in theological education of any kind (37%); the majority expresses a desire for at least some level of religious enrichment. This is especially true among practicing Christians. And while most churches do not, on their own, have capacity to create degree programs for knowledge-hungry Christians, these findings demonstrate widespread religious interest among both believers and everyday Americans—and may indicate an opportunity for churches to partner with Bible colleges, Christian universities or even educators in the congregation to meet these needs.

CHURCHES & COMMUNITY NEEDS

As part of *The State of Pastors* study, Barna also asked U.S. adults what needs in their community might be met by local churches. People could select all the options they believe apply to their community—and some people selected nearly all of them! Many Boomers, especially, seem convinced that churches are well-placed and uniquely equipped to meet many of their community's needs.

On the other hand, Millennials appear more skeptical about the role churches can or should play in their neighborhood; 16 percent say churches could provide "none of the above," compared to 11 percent of older adults. It may be that most Millennials believe only a few of these needs are particularly pressing for their own community—or perhaps their skepticism of churches and religious organizations is simply a higher hurdle to clear. Lending weight to this suggestion is the notably small percentage of Millennials who say "teaching the Bible / teaching about Jesus" is a need churches could meet; just one in five young adults says so (20%), compared to half of all Boomers (51%)

Overall, Americans believe churches could "feed the needy," provide "clothing for the needy," offer "spiritual guidance" and be "a place where everyone is accepted." Other needs include "activities for teens in the community," "shelter for the homeless" and "counseling services." But, as you can see on the following page, the generational spread on each of these is significant.

COMMUNITY NEEDS CHURCHES COULD MEET, BY GENERATION
% among U.S. adults

● all U.S. adults ● Millennials ● Gen-Xers ● Boomers ● Elders

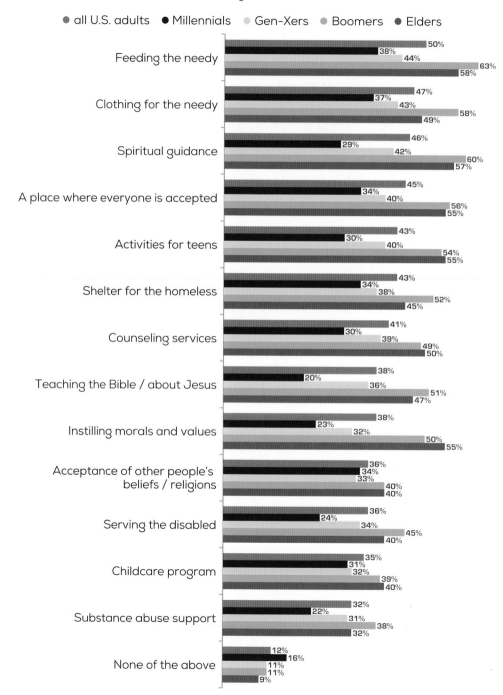

Feeding the needy
- 50%
- 38%
- 44%
- 63%
- 58%

Clothing for the needy
- 47%
- 37%
- 43%
- 58%
- 49%

Spiritual guidance
- 46%
- 29%
- 42%
- 60%
- 57%

A place where everyone is accepted
- 45%
- 34%
- 40%
- 56%
- 55%

Activities for teens
- 43%
- 30%
- 40%
- 54%
- 55%

Shelter for the homeless
- 43%
- 34%
- 38%
- 52%
- 45%

Counseling services
- 41%
- 30%
- 39%
- 49%
- 50%

Teaching the Bible / about Jesus
- 38%
- 20%
- 36%
- 51%
- 47%

Instilling morals and values
- 38%
- 23%
- 32%
- 50%
- 55%

Acceptance of other people's beliefs / religions
- 36%
- 34%
- 33%
- 40%
- 40%

Serving the disabled
- 36%
- 24%
- 34%
- 45%
- 40%

Childcare program
- 35%
- 31%
- 32%
- 39%
- 40%

Substance abuse support
- 32%
- 22%
- 31%
- 38%
- 32%

None of the above
- 12%
- 16%
- 11%
- 11%
- 9%

30. CHALLENGES

What is the toughest part about pastoring in today's culture?

Throughout *The State of Pastors* we've looked at aspects of their vocation that bring pastors joy, parts of their job for which they wish they'd been better prepared and the ministry tasks they find most frustrating. Zooming out from the specifics of their everyday responsibilities, what do church leaders say is their biggest challenge? What are the broader issues that sometimes make church leadership a test of trust and endurance? And how do leaders' perceptions of their greatest pastoral challenges square with Barna's findings on leading in complexity?

Using an open-ended, write-in question, Barna asked pastors, "What are the most challenging aspects of being a pastor in today's culture?"

A few common themes emerge from their answers, but the clearest takeaway is that different pastors find very different things a challenge. In a statistical tie are "juggling the demands of the job," "competing for people's time," "apathetic / uncommitted Christians" and "engaging younger generations," closely followed by "being relevant without conforming" and "making disciples." Pastors under 50, in particular, find that juggling job demands presents a challenge, and are somewhat more likely than older leaders to say apathetic Christians are the most challenging fact of their ministry. Pastors 50 and older, on the other hand, admit engaging younger generations is a challenge for them. In a similar vein, "keeping up with cultural changes" is uniquely challenging for leaders who have been in ministry for 30 years or longer.

There are a few small but significant differences between pastors of growing congregations and those with declining attendance. Leaders of shrinking churches tend to say "spectator /

DIFFERENT PASTORS FIND VERY DIFFERENT THINGS A CHALLENGE, FURTHER EVIDENCE THAT "COMPLEXITY" IS AN APT DESCRIPTION OF TODAY'S CULTURAL ECOSYSTEM

THE MOST CHALLENGING ASPECTS OF BEING A PASTOR TODAY

% among U.S. Protestant pastors

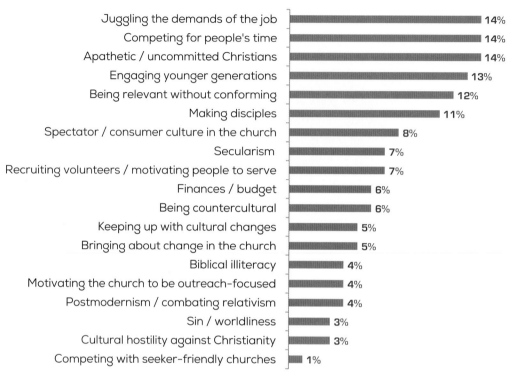

Juggling the demands of the job	14%
Competing for people's time	14%
Apathetic / uncommitted Christians	14%
Engaging younger generations	13%
Being relevant without conforming	12%
Making disciples	11%
Spectator / consumer culture in the church	8%
Secularism	7%
Recruiting volunteers / motivating people to serve	7%
Finances / budget	6%
Being countercultural	6%
Keeping up with cultural changes	5%
Bringing about change in the church	5%
Biblical illiteracy	4%
Motivating the church to be outreach-focused	4%
Postmodernism / combating relativism	4%
Sin / worldliness	3%
Cultural hostility against Christianity	3%
Competing with seeker-friendly churches	1%

n=357 U.S. Protestant pastors; total is greater than 100%
because pastors could offer more than one answer.

consumer culture within the church" is a particular challenge, while making disciples is a more urgent concern for pastors who lead growing churches.

Black senior pastors are more likely than their white colleagues to cite "recruiting volunteers / motivating people to serve" and "finances / budget" as challenges.

The wide array of answers suggests that the particularities of a pastor's ministry—facts on the ground that are not easily reduced to statistics—are a greater factor than his or her demographics when it comes to the challenges a pastor faces. Yes, there are a handful of statistically significant commonalities between pastors of similar age, ethnicity, region, ministry tenure and so on. But more remarkable is the immense range of concerns, further evidence that "complexity" is an apt description of the cultural ecosystem where pastors are working to cultivate faith that reseeds and reproduces in each new generation.

There are good reasons pastors are feeling challenged: because there are real factors at work that make leading God's people harder—or, at least, difficult in a different way. In the final section, Barna president David Kinnaman offers recommendations for how pastors can be resilient leaders in light of increasing complexity.

Q&A WITH GLENN PACKIAM

GLENN PACKIAM

Glenn Packiam is one of the associate senior pastors at New Life Church in Colorado Springs, Colorado, and the lead pastor of New Life Downtown, a congregation of New Life Church. He is author of *Discover the Mystery of Faith, LUCKY, Secondhand Jesus* and *Butterfly in Brazil*. He's also the writer of beloved New Life worship songs like "Your Name" and "My Savior Lives." Glenn holds a BA in Theological / Historical Studies, a Masters in Management and, after two years of graduate work at Fuller Theological Seminary, is pursuing doctoral research in theology at Durham University in the UK. Glenn, his wife, Holly, and their four children enjoy life in the shadow of the mighty Rocky Mountains.

Q: Pastors' top three challenges are juggling the demands of the job, competing for people's time and apathetic or uncommitted Christians. What is your advice to leaders who feel discouraged?

A: Let me say: I hear you! There are a few things that may help. First, be honest about your limitations. Discovering those limitations is the fruit of discovering who you are and what you do best. Tools like the Enneagram and Myers-Briggs are some of the ways you can deepen your journey of self-awareness to discover the unique ways God made you, and uncover the unique contributions you can make to your church. Once you know your limitations, you can recruit people to help (asking people to help is difficult, but is also a key component of making disciples) or decide to do fewer things as a church.

Speaking of doing fewer things, my second suggestion is to find ways to invite people into a different kind of rhythm. Rather than creating alternative experiences or events to the things they are already doing, our gift to our people is to show them a deeper way. We aren't trying to add to the clutter of their lives; we are trying to call them to an inward journey. Church can't be another thing to attend. Teaching a "rule of life" is one way to help people see the haphazard rhythms of their lives, the hollow goal that stands at the center and how everything can be reoriented around a different center.

Q: How do you think current challenges to pastors compare to those in the past? Are there any shared across time? Any especially unique to or pressing in this day and age?

A: I think our culture has no paradigm for what a pastor is, so we tend to borrow from existing paradigms. A few decades ago, a pastor was expected to be like a therapist or counselor.

Then, a pastor was to be an entrepreneur. In some circles, a pastor is supposed to be a revivalist or inspirational evangelist. Today, pastors are often looked at as social activists, creating change in their communities. These expectations are not only unfair; they are incorrect. We have to teach our people, show them and embody for them, what a pastor is and why it is a unique vocation.

That being said, the role of a pastor is contextually shaped. The role of a pastor must be adaptive to some degree to the context of the congregation. We are always, as Eugene Peterson wrote, paying attention to the particularities of the soil.

Most of us don't do ministry in a "parish" context, where a geographic community looks to a pastor as their priest, called upon when babies are born or loved ones are dying; instead, we are actively calling people to gather in worship, into a new kind of community and into a life of service. What's tricky is the people we are trying to reach and shepherd arrive with pre-existing notions of what it means to be a Christian. We're not working with a blank slate. This dynamic is more complex in our day because of the flurry of voices from social media, blogs, podcasts and so on with perceived authority derived from popularity. Many of our parishioners don't know how to sort out solid theological reflection from what isn't so, like it or not, our voice becomes just one of many Christian voices in their spiritual formation.

Q: How can pastors be better equipped for the emotional and empathetic weight of leadership?
A: Pastors can benefit from more training in the psychological dimensions of human behavior. I have been helped, for instance, by learning about attachment theory, the science behind addictions and the way emotions work—just to name a few topics. Becoming conversant in the social sciences can help us have an integrated spirituality that does not separate "spiritual things" from our humanity, or "theology" from "psychology."

However, most pastors will not, nor should we, become experts in these fields. That is why it can be useful to involve the counseling community in our congregation's care. That may mean referring people to a professional counselor after one or two meetings with them; and it could mean having counselors teach premarital classes or parenting sessions. People need more than an exegesis of Ephesians 5 to help their marriages. And yet all the techniques in the world, unmoored from the theology of what marriage is for, will prove hollow.

So, bringing the two worlds together—the social sciences, like psychology and sociology, with theology—can enrich our care for people. But that need not be the work of one super-pastor. Rather it will likely be the result of curating a team of pastors and counselors, staff people and lay people, who know how to work together.

LEADING IN COMPLEXITY

At least nine trends are creating a new ecosystem that will require adaptive leadership from pastors, lay leaders and denominational partners.

1.

DEMOGRAPHIC
Not only are Millennials the largest adult generation in terms of sheer numbers, they are also the most ethnically, culturally and spiritually diverse (unlike many of our churches).

2.

SOCIAL
Young people are generally going through the shaping experiences of adulthood at later ages than did previous generations—yet most of our churches are designed with families in mind.

3.

ECONOMIC
The economic pressures on middle-class and working families are being passed on to local churches, and the financial and ministry implications are immense.

4.

VOCATIONAL
The landscape of work is shifting toward a gig-oriented, multi-careering, freelance terrain, and there is profound need for a robust theology of vocational discipleship.

5.

INSTITUTIONAL
People get the information they want, when they want, for the price they want to pay. "Disintermediated institutions"—including churches—are no longer the sole mediators of knowledge, and pastors no longer the chief authority.

6.

LEGAL
Particularly when it comes to holding historically orthodox beliefs about human sexuality, Christian institutions are at increasing risk of running afoul of the law.

7.

DIGITAL
The "screen age" requires adaptive approaches to community and discipleship. "Digital Babylon" is an always-on, hyperlinked, immersive culture where Christians must learn to live and thrive as exiles.

8.

MORAL
Society's moral center is shifting away from external sources of authority (the Bible, Christian tradition) to the self: You look inside yourself to find what's best for you.

9.

SPIRITUAL
"Nones," or the religiously unaffiliated, are the fastest growing religious group in the nation. Nominal, cultural Christianity is no longer the "default position" of Americans—and this reality is challenging the Church to reevaluate faith formation.

RESILIENCE IN COMPLEXITY

by David Kinnaman

Culture is under constant reconstruction. The nine trends on the previous graphic are examples of powerful culture-building trends that are changing the way we live and lead. The team at Barna is committed to studying and assessing how these kinds of movements intersect to create complexity. Our objective is to help spiritual influencers understand the times and know what to do (see 1 Chron. 12:32), and we believe it's impossible to understand our times without getting a handle on today's trends.

Let's think together about how three of the preceding trends—the *institutional, moral* and *spiritual*—affect ministry. For pastors, the disintermediation of institutions means the traditional role of churches as a source of spiritual authority is increasingly removed from the minds of today's citizens. As society's moral center shifts away from external sources toward self-fulfillment, pastors' knowledge of the Scriptures and Christian orthodoxy appears irrelevant or even extreme. And the waning of nominal Christianity's cultural power means that, in order to follow Christ, Christians must swim against the current rather than going with the flow. In other words, if living as Christians is increasingly countercultural, then *pastoring* those Christians is a hard swim upstream, too.

While pastors are as important as ever in Christ's kingdom, in a society undergoing spiritual reconstruction they seem less significant. In the past, a career in ministry might have appealed to any leader who sought recognition and respect. Today, however, Christian ministers are as likely to be ignored and insulted as they are to be admired and revered. It's not a job for the thin-skinned or the weak of heart.

It's a job for the resilient.

After more than three decades studying churches in the U.S. and elsewhere, we at Barna believe the Christian community has, at times, focused too much on raising up strong, almost heroic leaders. But in their excellent book *Team of Teams*, General Stanley McChrystal (Ret.) and his coauthors contrast *robust*—another word for strong—with *resilient*. The pyramids at Giza are robust: big, impressive, immovable, unchangeable except by increments or an act of God. Yet given enough firepower, a single person could wipe them off the face of the earth. A forest, on the other hand, is resilient: at first glance, more vulnerable than the pyramids to a devastation-level event such as a wildfire or attack by an invasive parasite. But wait a decade or a century, and the forest is likely to have recovered—and the soil beneath the trees to be richer, as well.[32]

As church leaders in a time of unparalleled complexity, I believe we must seek to be more like forests and less like pyramids, able to adapt to or recover from whatever cultural wildfire or superbug comes along. In the introduction to this report, I touched on five traits of resilience uncovered by *The State of Pastors* research. A resilient leader:

- Prioritizes their own spiritual, emotional and physical needs
- Views challenges realistically
- Learns from their mistakes
- Considers alternate perspectives and new processes
- Expects that God is at work even in adverse situations

How can we cultivate the inner resources and outward behaviors that bear the fruit of resilience? Here are a few ideas, along with some discussion questions to get you thinking and your team talking.

SELF-LEADERSHIP: BEING A RESILIENT PERSON

In many ways, pastors are already some of the most resilient humans on the planet. *The State of Pastors* shows that most church leaders are content in their home life, joyful in pursuit of God, managing their finances well, maintaining mental and emotional equilibrium, open to learning new things and confident as ever in their ministry calling. Pastors and those who support them, whether relationally or institutionally, should be encouraged that their work thus far is paying off, and renew their commitments to fortify these areas of strength.

Yet the research also raises some red flags. The number of pastors at some risk of burnout, relationship troubles or spiritual problems are cause for concern. Because their calling is so central to their identity, it can be tempting for pastors to rank the business of leading and serving ahead of soul care and intimate relationships—but doing the former well (leading, serving) depends on prioritizing the latter (soul care, relationships). As Pete Scazzero says in his Q&A with Barna, "Our first work as spiritual leaders is to live *congruently* . . . Our roles and our souls must remain connected; this is our primary work and the greatest gift we can give to others."

In this age of distraction and celebrity, pastors and their networks of support must consider what it looks like to practice *effective self-leadership*. The "self" in "self-leadership" should not imply that spiritual leaders are or should be on their own—far from it. It's just shorthand for the inner experiences and closest relationships that make pastors who they are, the fundamental stuff of being human. Amply investing in these aspects of life is effective self-leadership.

- Who is helping you keep tabs on your inner life, including your mental health and spiritual vitality? What do you need in order to grow in these areas?

- How is your physical health? What is one way to take better care of the body that allows you to do all you do, including ministry?

- Are you feeling anxiety related to money? How can you better steward your finances and practice generosity?

- How are things going in your family, in your marriage? What is your next step to deepen or heal those relationships? Who can help?

- Take stock of your friendships—how deep are they, really? What will you do to invest more of your true self into life-giving friendships?

- Who speaks truth into your life and how regularly transparent are you with them? Is better accountability a matter of more frequent mentoring or a different mentor altogether, or both?

- At the heart of personal resilience is intimacy with Jesus—in what ways are you practicing his presence and inviting him to transform your life?

 CHURCH LEADERSHIP: CREATING A RESILIENT TEAM

Reviewing the findings from this part of the research, it strikes me that most of the problem areas of *effective church leadership* are best addressed by understanding the difference between technical solutions and adaptive leadership. (Ron Heifetz's writing on adaptive leadership is must reading for church leaders.[33]) Technical solutions are well and good if returning to the status quo is the ultimate goal. A cast and sling, for example, are technical solutions designed to return a broken arm to its former condition. Upon completion of the healing process, everything is "as good as new." A lot of churches try to solve problems using this mindset: *How can we get back to where things used to be?*

But an adaptive problem is a level up. Its very nature is complex. Amputation of a limb, for instance, requires adapting to a new reality; there's no returning to the status quo. Adaptive leadership recognizes there is no going back to simpler times; complexity is now reality.

In churches, as in life, there are many technical glitches, but the most vexing problems are adaptive. Yet we often try to fix adaptive problems with technical solutions. Just as an example, we might think raising up church leaders among the next generation is merely a matter of finding that one "perfect" young leader—but ministry succession is not a technical problem.

One of the most significant features of an adaptive problem is that *we must change* in order to face the challenge effectively. Pouring into the lives of younger leaders changes a pastor. So does casting and living into an expansive vision of what pastoring is and can be. Expanding the leadership team to include gifted young people—and expanding our vision of ministry calling to include the networks where people live and work—will certainly require a senior leader to change.

Another one of those adaptations is learning to lead in the context of teams. More so than ever, churches need to embody a *team of teams* approach. George Barna's work has long highlighted the need for different *types* of leaders to come alongside each other to build great organizations and healthy churches. His book *A Fish Out of Water* describes four distinct aspects of leadership: Directing Leaders, Strategic Leaders, Operational Leaders and Team-Building Leaders.[34] Healthy organizations have all four, and since no one person can embody all these qualities, a team is the best option.

"Teams of teams" in your context might mean connecting young and old, paid ministry staff and lay leaders, singles and marrieds, and so on. For many churches it will mean creating more deeply spiritual partnerships—highly focused on prayer, for example—between pastors and elders. Taking nothing away from the importance of God's intention for faithful *individual leaders*, churches need better approaches to solving problems, building disciples and serving our communities *as teams*, not as lone wolves. It's Acts-like work: deploying groups of people into the world for the sake of Jesus.

Relatedly, one of the most glaring challenges facing the Church today is the aging of today's pastors. This is an urgent, adaptive-level problem that will require us to change. Doubling down on a team approach to leadership will help us adapt to this looming potential crisis *and* help us engage young leaders who may be looking elsewhere for opportunities to make a kingdom impact.

Creating better teams is adaptive leadership, and it is an important key to effective church leadership in this era of complexity.

- Is there an area where your mentoring of younger leaders has fallen short? What needs to change to fill the gap?
- What is working well in your church that should be continued or could be enhanced? Who needs to be acknowledged or recognized for their contributions to what's working?
- How could the pastoral staff and elder team become better at problem solving together, distinguishing between technical and adaptive problems?
- What kinds of spiritual, relational or intellectual tools might be necessary to handle more complicated questions and problems?
- Are leaders demonstrating both intellectual humility and courageous conviction? What must change to bring those into healthy tension?
- In what ways have you missed the chance to bring spiritual practices to your team leadership—such as praying as a team of leaders?

- Are you or your team more concerned with preserving your present reality and traditional approach than with adapting together to a complex future?
- How can your team focus on Jesus as the object of your devotion and the purpose of all you do?

CULTURAL LEADERSHIP: FORMING A RESILIENT COMMUNITY

While their cultural influence may never reach that of a C. S. Lewis or a Reinhold Niebuhr, called and committed pastors remain absolutely indispensable. Thanks to the Internet, information is cheap but wisdom is at an all-time premium—and a society hurtling full-speed towards a cliff needs all the wisdom it can get, even if it mocks the worker in the orange vest waving SLOW and CAUTION signs. How can pastors to exercise *effective cultural leadership*?

First, teach your congregation how to engage in meaningful conversations—and model it, too. In order for the Church to be a resilient, effective minority in today's society, we're going to have to get past our conversational barriers. Barna has found that evangelicals are among the most conversationally challenged segments, meaning they feel least equipped to have a meaningful conversation with someone who believes differently from them.[35] And as this report shows, pastors admit to feeling unprepared to teach people how to have those conversations.

The discomfort caused by complexity tempts many people to pick a hill, plant a flag and hurl down curses on anyone who doesn't agree, just to feel a little less uncomfortable and a little more righteous. Social media makes this temptation almost irresistible. However, if changing minds and hearts—and allowing *our* hearts and minds to be transformed by Christ—is the ultimate goal, we must find another way. Meaningful conversations happen when we listen, understand, reflect and respond with kindness and conviction. It is nearly a lost art—and is at the heart of evangelism and discipleship—so if you and your congregation can revive the craft of meaningful conversation, people you don't expect will want to listen and be heard.

Second, in an era of complexity, churches can become learning communities. What I mean by "learning" is resilient heart-mind-soul-and-strength formation that makes us new creations in Jesus. The typical churchgoer comes to church fewer weekends per year than in the past, and a few sermons a month are not sufficient to form people in the ways of Jesus—especially not in a culture that pummels people with warped ideas about life and how to live it. In many ways, learning—which includes both knowledge acquisition and practice-making-perfect—is the very essence of Christian discipleship: learning the ways of God; learning to live in light of Christ's rule and reign; and learning to depend on and be guided by the Holy Spirit.

It is remarkable that, despite so much indifference to Christianity and the waning cultural influence of pastors, there is still a strong desire among most people to *learn*. In a complex, accelerated culture, people have many questions. How can your church become a learning community that helps people to develop cultural discernment? Pastors enjoy preaching, which is certainly one essential part of learning. But it's not the only way people today should be formed. Preaching is not sufficient to bring about whole-life learning (heart, mind, soul and strength) in a society of distracted, self-centered people for whom the echoes of Christianity are muted. Don't get me wrong: Preaching is important. But it's less sufficient today to exclusively do the job of faith formation. (Refer to point number one on the importance of meaningful conversations!) Our faith speaks to the everyday issues of life: money, sexuality, relationships, work, race relations, entertainment and so on. And these are topics on which informed Christians—including pastors—can speak meaningfully into today's cultural context.

Third, take the long view. It's far too easy to get caught up in the headlines of the day and begin to believe today's complex crisis is all there is. It's not. The Holy Spirit has sustained the Church for a couple thousand years now and shows no sign of calling it a day. Let's trust the Spirit's sustaining power not to quit, and prepare for the future. What will the North American church need in 50 or 100 years? What institutions or practices should we create or revitalize in order to serve those sisters and brothers of the future? Pastors are ideally situated to plant the seeds, because the youngest members of your church *are* those sisters and brothers of the future—and you are forming them today to lead the Church and the world tomorrow.

- When your church serves your community, how well are you listening? How can you make conversations more meaningful?
- How can we tackle critically important issues—things like race, poverty, sexuality, work and so on—through our churches?
- How can our churches develop rich countercultural patterns of belief and behavior that stand as a witness to society?
- Does your church practice prayer in the pattern of Jeremiah 29, praying for the peace and prosperity of our post-Christian society?
- What needs to change in your thinking about formation and pedagogy in order for whole-life learning to define your church community?
- How can Jesus take center stage in all your church does as you seek to be a counterculture for the common good?

Taking the long view also means believing Jesus when he says the gates of hell will not prevail against the Church we inherited from the apostles. Now *that's* resilience!

 APPENDIX

A. NOTES

1. George Barna, *Today's Pastors: A Revealing Look at What Pastors Are Saying About Themselves, Their Peers and the Pressures They Face* (Ventura, CA: Regal Books, 1993). All 1992 data from this source.
2. U.S. Bureau of the Census, Current Population Reports, Series P20–484. https://www.census.gov/prod/1/pop/p20-484.pdf (accessed October 2016).
3. U.S. Bureau of the Census, "America's Families and Living Arrangements: 2014). http://www.census.gov/hhes/families/data/cps2014A.html (accessed October 2016).
4. Median 1992 incomes adjusted for inflation. http://www.usinflationcalculator.com/ (accessed October 2016).
5. Cynthia Woolever and Deborah Bruce, *Leadership That Fits Your Church: What Kind of Pastor for What Kind of Congregation* (Atlanta, GA: Chalice Press, 2012), pp. 12–13.
6. Steven H. Chapman, Mitchell P. LaPlante and Gail Wilensky, "Life Expectancy and Health Status of the Aged," *Social Security Bulletin*, Oct. 1986, vol. 49, no. 10. https://www.ssa.gov/policy/docs/ssb/v49n10/v49n10p24.pdf (accessed December 2016). See also https://www.google.com/publicdata/explore?ds=d5bncppjof8f9_&met_y=sp_dyn_le00_in-&idim=country:USA:CAN:GBR&hl=en&dl=en (accessed December 2016).
7. Jackson W. Carroll, "First- and Second-Career Clergy: Some Comparisons and Questions," *Pulpit & Pew*, 2002. http://pulpitandpew.org/first-and-second-career-clergy-some-comparisons-and-questions (accessed December 2016).
8. Dave Carpenter, "Many Clergy Ill-Prepared for Retirement," *USA Today*, June 5, 2010. http://usatoday30.usatoday.com/news/religion/2010-06-05-clergy-retire_N.htm (accessed December 2016).
9. G. Barna, *Today's Pastors*, p. 60.
10. U.S. Bureau of the Census, "Selected Characteristics of People 15 and Over by Total Money Income, Work Experience, Race, Hispanic Origin and Sex," PINC-01. http://www.census.gov/data/tables/time-series/demo/income-poverty/cps-pinc/pinc-01.html (accessed October 2016).
11. Barna Group, *Church Startups and Money: The Myths and Realities of Church Planters and Finances* (Ventura, CA: Barna Group, 2016), p. 25.
12. Barna Group, *The Porn Phenomenon: The Impact of Pornography in the Digital Age* (Ventura, CA: Barna Group, 2016), pp. 80–83.
13. Ibid., p. 43. Twelve percent of U.S. women 25 and older report seeking out pornography up to once or twice a month, compared to 47 percent of men.
14. E. J. Krumrei Mancuso and S. V. Rouse, "The Development and Validation of the Comprehensive Intellectual Humility Scale," *Journal of Personality Assessment*, Nov. 2015, pp. 209–221. doi.org/10.1080/00223891.2015.1068174 (accessed October 2016).
15. B. M. DePaulo, K. Charlton, H. Cooper, J. J. Lindsay and L. Muhlenbruck, "The Accuracy-Confidence Correlation in the Detection of Deception," *Personality and Social Psychology Review*, Nov. 1997, vol. 1, no. 4, pp. 346–357. doi:10.1207/s15327957pspr0104_5 (accessed October 2016); S. Sporer, S. Penrod, D. Read and B. Cutler, "Choosing, Confidence and Accuracy: A Meta-Analysis of the Confidence-Accuracy Relation in Eyewitness Identification Studies, *Psychological Bulletin*, Nov. 1995, vol. 118. doi:10.1037/0033-2909.118.3.315 (accessed October 2016).
16. Krumrei Mancuso and Rouse, pp. 209–221.
17. E. J. Krumrei Mancuso, "Intellectual Humility and Prosocial Values: Direct and Mediated Effects," *Journal of Positive Psychology*, April 2016. doi: 10.1080/17439760.2016.1167938 (accessed October 2016).
18. Simon Sinek, *Start with Why: How Great Leaders Inspire Everyone to Take Action* (New York: Portfolio, 2009).
19. Barna Group, *Transforming Scotland: The State of Christianity, Faith and the Church in Scotland* (Ventura, CA: Barna Group, 2015), p. 55.
20. Neil Patel, "90% of Startups Fail: Here's What You Need to Know About the 10%," Forbes.com, Jan. 16, 2015. http://www.forbes.com/sites/neilpatel/2015/01/16/90-of-startups-will-fail-heres-what-you-need-to-know-about-the-10/#4d5d7cbe55e1 (accessed November 2016).
21. Thom S. Rainer, "Seven Ways Pastors (and Others) Can Develop Thicker Skin," ThomRainer.com, October 26, 2013. http://thomrainer.com/2013/10/seven-ways-pastors-and-others-can-develop-thicker-skin/ (accessed October 2016).

22. Kristen Doerer, "U.S. Has a Lousy Work-Life Balance," *PBS NewsHour*, July 3, 2015. http://www.pbs.org/newshour/updates/u-s-lousy-work-life-balance/ (accessed October 2016).

23. G. Barna, *Today's Pastors*, pp. 65–67.

24. George Barna and David Kinnaman, Gen. Editors, *Churchless: Understanding Today's Unchurched and How to Connect with Them* (Carol Stream, IL: Tyndale House Publishers, 2014).

25. David Kinnaman and Gabe Lyons, *Good Faith: Being a Christian When Society Thinks You're Irrelevant and Extreme* (Grand Rapids, MI: Baker Books, 2016).

26. To be addressed in Barna's forthcoming *Faith Leaders on Religious Liberty* report.

27. Dallas Willard, *Knowing Christ Today* (New York: HarperOne, 2009), p. 198.

28. Barna Group, "Religious Beliefs Have Greatest Influence on Voting Decisions," Research release Oct. 27, 2016. https://www.barna.com/research/religious-beliefs-have-greatest-influence-on-voting-decisions/ (accessed November 2016).

29. See *The Bible in America: The Changing Landscape of Bible Perceptions and Engagement* (Ventura, CA: Barna, 2016).

30. For an overview of the biblical and historic understanding of these ideas, see Theology of Work Project, "Calling & Vocation: Overview," TheologyOfWork.org. https://www.theologyofwork.org/key-topics/vocation-overview-article (accessed November 2016).

31. Kenneth L. Woodward, *Getting Religion: Faith, Culture, and Politics from the Age of Eisenhower to the Era of Obama* (New York: Convergent Books, 2016), p. 102.

32. Stanley McChrystal, Tantum Collins, David Silverman and Chris Fussell, *Team of Teams: New Rules of Engagement for a Complex World* (New York: Portfolio / Penguin, 2015).

33. Ronald A. Heifetz, Marty Linsky and Alexander Grashow, *The Practice of Adaptive Leadership: Tools and Tactics for Changing Your Organization and the World* (Cambridge, MA: Harvard Review Press, 2009).

34. George Barna, *A Fish Out of Water: 9 Strategies Effective Leaders Use to Get You Back into the Flow* (Nashville, TN: Integrity, 2002).

35. Kinnaman and Lyons, *Good Faith*, pp. 43–45.

B. DEFINITIONS

U.S. PROTESTANT PASTORS

Age
Under 50
50 and older

Church Size
Small: less than 100 adult attenders
Midsize: 100 to 249 adult attenders
Large: 250 or more attenders

Church Tenure
1 to 3 years at current church
4 to 9 years at current church
10 years or more at current church

Compensation
Less than $40,000 per year
$40,000 to $60,000 per year
$60,000 or more per year

Denominations
Mainline: pastors from Protestant denominations such as American Baptist Churches USA, the Episcopal Church, Evangelical Lutheran Church of America, United Church of Christ, United Methodist Church and Presbyterian Church USA

Non-mainline: pastors from Protestant traditions such as charismatic / Pentecostal churches, the Southern Baptist Convention, churches in the Wesleyan-Holiness tradition and non-denominational churches not included in mainline

Education

Attended seminary

Did not attend seminary

Ethnicity

Black: choose "black or African American" from a list of ethnic identities

Pastors of color: combined segment of all non-white pastors

White: choose "white" from a list of ethnic identities

Growth Trajectory

Growing: pastor reports growth in attendance since 12 months ago

Flat: pastor reports unchanged attendance since 12 months ago

Declining: pastor reports decline in attendance since 12 months ago

Ministry Tenure

Less than 15 years in full-time paid ministry (total)

15 to 29 years in full-time paid ministry (total)

30 ore more years in full-time paid ministry (total)

Risk Metrics

Burnout risk is assessed using 11 factors from *The State of Pastors* research (see page 21 for a list). A pastor is low risk if they do not meet any of the factors; medium risk if they meet criteria for one of the factors; and high risk if they meet three or more of the factors.

Relationship risk is assessed using seven factors from the study (see page 21 for a list). A pastor is considered low risk if they do not meet any of the factors; medium risk if they meet one or two factors; and high risk if they meet three or more factors.

Spiritual risk is assessed using four factors from the study (see page 21 for a list). A pastor is considered low risk if they do not meet criteria for any of the factors; medium risk if they meet one to two factors; and high risk if they meet three or more factors.

Satisfaction Segments

Vocational satisfaction: based on the question, "Overall, how satisfied are you with your vocation as a pastor?" Those who selected "very satisfied" (72%) are in the "very satisfied" segment; those who selected "somewhat," "not too" or "not at all satisfied" (28%) are in the "less satisfied" segment.

Satisfaction with current church ministry: based on the question, "How satisfied are you with your ministry at your current church?" Those who selected "very satisfied" (53%) are in the "very satisfied" segment; those who selected "somewhat," "not too" or "not at all satisfied" (47%) are in the "less satisfied" segment.

U.S. ADULTS

Bible Engagement

Bible engaged: A person who is "engaged" has a high view of scripture and reads the Bible four or more times per week. They view the Bible as 1) the *actual* or 2) the *inspired* word of God with no errors, or as 3) the *inspired* word of God with some errors. They also read, use or listen to the Bible four times a week or more.

Bible friendly: Like the engaged, the "friendly" person holds a high view of scripture, but reads it fewer than four times in a week.

Bible neutral: Someone who is "neutral" has a lower, but not negative, view of scripture. This person neither chooses the top two statements about the Bible (i.e., the highest views) nor the most skeptical statement. They tend to pick "middle options" in the survey. Rarely or never read the Bible.

Bible skeptic: Someone who is a "skeptic" selects the statement in the survey that reflects the lowest view of the Bible—that it is "just another book of teachings written by men." In other words, there is no God "behind" the Bible. Rarely or never read the Bible.

Churched Segments

Churched: have attended a worship service within the past six months
Unchurched: have not attended a worship service within the past six months
    De-churched: unchurched who previously attended church
    Never churched: unchurched who have never attended church

Education

High school or less: have not attended college

Some college: attended college but do not have a four-year degree; includes those who graduated from a trade school

College graduate: received a four-year degree or higher

Ethnicity

Black: choose "black or African-American" from a list of ethnic identities

Hispanic: choose "Hispanic" from a list of ethnic identities

People of color: combined segment of all non-white respondents

White: choose "white" from a list of ethnic identities

Faith Segments

Self-identified Christians choose "Christian" from a list of religious affiliations.

Practicing Christians are self-identified Christians who strongly agree their faith is very important in their life and have attended a worship service within the past month.

Non-practicing Christians are self-identified Christians who do not meet the "practicing" criteria.

Evangelicals have made a personal commitment to Jesus Christ that is still important in their life today and believe that, when they die, they will go to heaven because they have confessed their sins and accepted Jesus as their Savior (Barna's "born again" criteria) and meet seven other conditions: saying their faith is very important in their life today; believing they have a personal responsibility to share their religious beliefs about Christ with non-Christians; believing that Satan exists; believing that Jesus Christ lived a sinless life on earth; asserting that the Bible is accurate in all that it teaches; believing that eternal salvation is possible only through grace, not works; and describing God as the all-knowing, all-powerful, perfect deity who created the universe and still rules it today. Being classified as an evangelical is not dependent on church attendance or the denominational affiliation of the church attended. Respondents are not asked to describe themselves as "evangelical."

Other faith describes people who choose a religion other than Christianity from a list of religious affiliations.

No faith or *no religious affiliation* are atheists or agnostics, or choose "none of the above" from a list of religious affiliations.

Generations

Millennials: born 1984 to 2002

Gen-Xers: born 1965 to 1983

Boomers: born 1946 to 1964

Elders: born before 1946

Income

Lower-income: less than $50,000 per year

Middle-income: $50,000 to less than $100,000 per year

Higher-income: $100,000 or more per year

C. METHODOLOGIES

The data in this report originated from a series of research studies conducted by Barna Group of Ventura, California.

Dates	Audience	Collection method	Sample size	Sampling error	Funded by
2006–2016	Senior pastors	Aggregate database*	14,033	±0.8	Barna
Oct 2016	Senior pastors	Online	600	±3.9	Pepperdine University
Dec 2015–Jan 2016	Senior pastors	Phone	606	±3.9	Maclellan Foundation
Apr–Dec 2015	Senior pastors	Online and phone	900	±3.1	Pepperdine University
June–July 2014	Senior pastors	Online and phone	1,286	±2.6	Maclellan Foundation
May 2012	Senior pastors	Phone	603	±3.9	Barna
July–Aug 2016	U.S. adults	Online	1,000	±2.9	Association for Biblical Higher Education (ABHE)
Apr 2016	U.S. adults	Online	1,097	±2.8	Barna
Jan–Feb 2016	U.S. adults	Online and phone	2,008	±2.0	American Bible Society
Apr–May 2015	U.S. adults	Online	1,025	±2.9	Barna
Aug 2014	U.S. Millennials	Online	1,000	±2.9	Barna, American Bible Society, InterVarsity

* includes phone and online.

Protestant senior pastors, whether interviewed by phone or online, were recruited from publicly available church listings covering 90 percent of U.S. churches that have a physical address and a listed phone number or email address. Churches selected for inclusion were called up to five times at different times of the day to increase the probability of successful contact. Data were minimally weighted to match church characteristics from the National Congregation Study (by Association of Statisticians of American Religious Bodies) for denominational affiliation, church size and region.

Interviews with U.S. adults were conducted online and by telephone. All telephone interviews were conducted by Barna Group. All households were selected for inclusion in the sample using a random-digit dial technique, which allows every telephone household in the nation to have an equal and known probability of selection. Households selected for inclusion in the survey sample received multiple callbacks to increase the probability of obtaining a representative distribution of adults. Between 20 and 40 percent of telephone interviewing was conducted on cell phones.

For pastor and U.S. adult surveys, regional quotas were used to ensure that sufficient population dispersion was achieved. There were also minimum and maximum ranges placed on the distribution of respondents within several demographic variables that were tracked during the field process to ensure that statistical weighting would not be excessive. When a particular attribute reached one of the parameters, the sampling selection process was varied to preclude individuals who did not meet the necessary demographic criterion, with the interviewer seeking a person from the same church or household who fit the desired criterion.

Online interviews were conducted using an online research panel called KnowledgePanel® based on probability sampling that covers both the online and offline populations in the U.S. The panel members are randomly recruited by telephone and by self-administered mail and web surveys. Households are provided with access to the Internet and hardware if needed. Unlike other Internet research that covers only individuals with Internet access who volunteer for research, this process uses a dual sampling frame that includes both listed and unlisted phone numbers, telephone and non-telephone households, and cell-phone-only households. The panel is not limited to current Web users or computer owners. All potential panelists are randomly selected to join the KnowledgePanel; unselected volunteers are not able to join.

Once data was collected, minimal statistical weights were applied to several demographic variables to more closely correspond to known national averages.

When researchers describe the accuracy of survey results, they usually provide the estimated amount of "sampling error." This refers to the degree of possible inaccuracy that could be attributed to interviewing a group of people that is not completely representative of the population from which they were drawn. See the table for maximum sampling error. There is a range of other errors that can influence survey results (e.g., biased question wording, question sequencing, inaccurate recording of responses, inaccurate data tabulation, etc.)—errors whose influence on the findings cannot be statistically estimated. Barna makes every effort to overcome these possible errors at every stage of research.

ACKNOWLEDGEMENTS

Barna Group offers our heartfelt thanks and deep appreciation to Dale and Rita Brown, Tod Brown and the Moriah Foundation, who sponsored *The State of Pastors* research, and to our incomparable partners at Pepperdine University: Andrew Benton, Dyron Daughrity, Rick Gibson, Ronald Highfield, Sara Jackson, Elizabeth Krumrei Mancuso, David Lemley, Michael Menichetti, Joella Michaels, Ronald Phillips and Daniel Rodriguez.

Barna also wishes to thank the contributors to *The State of Pastors*: David Bailey, Bobby Gruenewald, Jim Hawkins, Sharon Hoover, Elizabeth Krumrei Mancuso, Terry Linhart, Glenn Packiam, Svetlana Papazov and Pete Scazzero. We are honored by your participation in this project and thankful for all God continues to do through your work.

The research team for this study is David Kinnaman, Inga Dahlstadt, Aly Hawkins, Traci Hochmuth and Pam Jacob. Mark Matlock, Preston Sprinkle and Victoria Loorz contributed analysis and insights. Under the editorial direction of Roxanne Stone, the writing team for *The State of Pastors* is Aly Hawkins, Cory Maxwell-Coghlan and Alyce Youngblood, with additional contributions from Joyce Chiu, Elliott Haught and Sarah Ngu. The design team is Judson Collier, Chaz Russo and Rob Williams. Brenda Usery managed production.

The State of Pastors team thanks our Barna colleagues Amy Brands, Chrisandra Bolton, Matt Carobini, Bill Denzel, Brooke Hempell, Jill Kinnaman, Elaine Klautzsch, Steve McBeth, Elise Miller, Josh Pearce, Megan Pritchett, Caitlin Schuman, Todd Sorenson, Sara Tandon and Todd White.

ABOUT THE PROJECT PARTNERS

Barna Group is a research firm dedicated to providing actionable insights on faith and culture, with a particular focus on the Christian church. Barna has conducted more than one million interviews in the course of hundreds of studies over more than three decades, and has become a go-to source for organizations that want to better understand a complex and changing world from a faith perspective. Barna's clients and partners include a broad range of academic institutions, churches, nonprofits and businesses, such as Alpha, the Templeton Foundation, Fuller Seminary, the Bill and Melinda Gates Foundation, Maclellan Foundation, DreamWorks Animation, Focus Features, Habitat for Humanity, The Navigators, NBC-Universal, the ONE Campaign, eHarmony, Paramount Pictures, the Salvation Army, Walden Media, Sony and World Vision. The firm's studies are frequently quoted by major media outlets such as *The Economist*, BBC, CNN, *USA Today*, the *Wall Street Journal*, Fox News, Huffington Post, *The New York Times* and the *Los Angeles Times*. *www.Barna.com*

Founded in 1937, **Pepperdine University** is an independent Christian university located 30 miles west of Los Angeles in scenic Malibu, California. The university enrolls approximately 7,300 students in its undergraduate school, Seaver College, the School of Law, the Graziadio School of Business and Management, the Graduate School of Education and Psychology, and the School of Public Policy. Pepperdine is committed to the highest standards of academic excellence and Christian values, where students are strengthened for lives of purpose, service and leadership. *www.Pepperdine.edu*

RESOURCES FOR CHURCH LEADERS

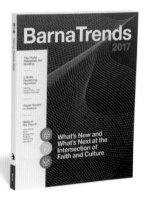

Barna Trends
Barna Trends 2017 puts essential information at your fingertips and in context and consolidates and interprets the raw data behind ongoing cultural, religious and political shifts

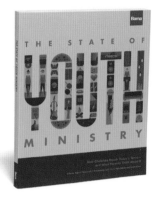

State of Youth Ministry
For pastors and parents to help them understand each other's hopes and expectations in order to work better together making young disciples who follow the way of Jesus

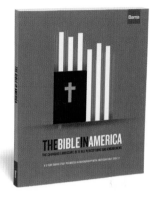

The Bible in America
The Bible in America offers analysis, insights and encouragement to leaders who want to understand Scripture engagement today and how to cultivate faith that lasts in an ever-changing world.

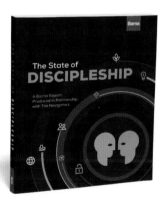

State of Discipleship
Based on a study commissioned by the Navigators, this monograph looks at how effectively the Church is making disciples and where there is need for better models.

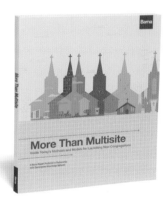

More Than Multisite
A comprehensive tool to help churches minimize the challenges of launching additional congregations so they can stay on mission as they grow

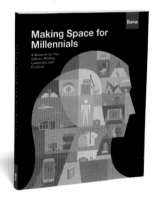

Making Space for Millennials
A handbook for designing culture, ministry, leadership and facilities with Millennials in mind. Create connections with Millennials in your church, school or organization